An Apologetic Journey: Exploring Christianity

Daniel Sanjurjo

Published by Inspire Christian, 2024.

While every precaution has been taken in the preparation of this book, the publisher assumes no responsibility for errors or omissions, or for damages resulting from the use of the information contained herein.

AN APOLOGETIC JOURNEY: EXPLORING CHRISTIANITY

First edition. June 26, 2024.

ISBN: 979-8227920409

Written by Daniel Sanjurjo.

Table of Contents

Dedication:

To Milagros and Fior,

Your unwavering support and love have been my guiding light.
This book is dedicated to you both, with all my heart.

Introduction:
On the Quest for Understanding: Exploring Challenges to Faith

Have you ever grappled with questions about faith? Does the existence of suffering, the vastness of science, or the diversity of religious beliefs challenge your core beliefs? If you're on a journey of faith, you're not alone.

This book delves into the common challenges that people face in a world seemingly at odds with traditional faith. We'll explore the problem of evil and suffering, the scientific advancements that sometimes clash with religious teachings, the rise of pluralism and relativism, and the ongoing debate about the role of reason and faith.

But this book isn't just about challenges. It's also about navigating them. We'll explore different apologetic approaches to defend your beliefs, cultivate intellectual humility for deeper understanding, and develop the crucial skills of listening and empathy for meaningful conversations about faith.

Whether you're seeking to strengthen your own faith, engage thoughtfully with those of differing beliefs, or simply embark on a quest for greater understanding, this book equips you with the tools you need. So, open your mind, embrace the questions, and join us on this exploration of the complexities of faith in the modern world.

Apologetics (pronounced uh-pa-lo-get-iks) is the discipline within religion concerned with defending religious doctrines through systematic reasoning and argument. In other words, it's the study of how to explain, justify, and defend your faith. Here's a breakdown of the concept:

Core Function:

● **Defense of Beliefs:** Apologetics aims to provide a reasoned defense of religious beliefs, addressing challenges and critiques from various perspectives.

Historical Context:

● **Early Christian Apologists:** The term originated with early Christians who defended their faith against persecution and philosophical attacks in the Roman Empire.

Approaches to Apologetics:

There are various approaches apologists take, some emphasizing reason and evidence, while others focus on personal experience or the transformative power of faith. Here are a few common types:

● **Classical Apologetics:** This approach uses logic, philosophy, and evidence (like historical records) to establish the existence of God and the truth claims of a religion.

● **Evidential Apologetics:** This approach focuses on using scientific evidence, historical data, and philosophical arguments to support religious beliefs.

● **Experiential Apologetics:** This approach emphasizes the role of personal experiences and the transformative power of faith in apologetic arguments.

● **Presuppositional Apologetics:** This unique approach argues that non-Christian worldviews are inherently illogical and instead focuses on exposing their inconsistencies.

Goals of Apologetics:

● **Strengthen Faith:** Apologetics can help believers strengthen their own faith by providing a deeper understanding of the reasons behind their beliefs.

● **Address Challenges:** It equips believers to address questions and doubts, along with critiques of their faith from outside perspectives.

● **Promote Faith:** Apologetics can be a tool for promoting faith to others by presenting a reasoned and persuasive case for religious belief.

Importance of Apologetics:

In a world with diverse belief systems and increasing secularism, apologetics can be a valuable tool for those who want to thoughtfully defend and explain their faith.

Apologetics, derived from the Greek word "apologia," meaning a defense, is the systematic defense of religious doctrines through logical arguments and evidence. In the context of Christianity, apologetics involves providing reasoned justifications for belief in God, the validity of Scripture, and the truth claims of the Christian faith.

In our increasingly secular and pluralistic world, the importance of apologetics cannot be overstated. It serves several crucial purposes:

a) Strengthening the faith of believers by addressing doubts and questions b) Equipping Christians to engage in meaningful dialogue with non-believers c) Presenting a rational case for Christianity to skeptics and seekers d) Countering misconceptions and criticisms of the Christian faith

This chapter will explore the foundations of apologetics, its biblical basis, and its relevance in contemporary society.

While the term "apologetics" itself doesn't appear in the Bible, the practice is firmly rooted in Scripture. Several key verses support and encourage believers to engage in apologetics:

a) 1 Peter 3:15 - "But in your hearts revere Christ as Lord. Always be prepared to give an answer to everyone who asks you to give the reason for the hope that you have. But do this with gentleness and respect."

This verse is often considered the cornerstone of Christian apologetics. It emphasizes the importance of being ready to explain and defend one's faith, while also highlighting the manner in which this should be done - with gentleness and respect.

b) Acts 17:2-3 - "As was his custom, Paul went into the synagogue, and on three Sabbath days he reasoned with them from the Scriptures, explaining and proving that the Messiah had to suffer and rise from the dead."

This passage illustrates Paul's apologetic approach, using reason and evidence to support his claims about Jesus as the Messiah.

c) Jude 3 - "Dear friends, although I was very eager to write to you about the salvation we share, I felt compelled to write and urge you to contend for the faith that was once for all entrusted to God's holy people."

Jude encourages believers to actively defend and contend for their faith, suggesting an apologetic stance.

Examples of apologetics in the Bible include:

1. Moses defending God's actions to Pharaoh (Exodus 5-12)
2. Elijah's contest with the prophets of Baal (1 Kings 18)
3. Jesus' responses to critics and skeptics (e.g., Matthew 22:15-22)
4. Paul's speech at the Areopagus (Acts 17:22-34)

These biblical examples demonstrate that apologetics has been an integral part of faith throughout history, providing a model for contemporary Christians to follow.

The Biblical Basis for Apologetics

The practice of apologetics, while not explicitly named in Scripture, is fundamentally rooted in biblical teachings and exemplified throughout both the Old and New Testaments. This section will explore the scriptural foundations of apologetics, examining key verses, analyzing biblical examples, and discussing the theological implications of these passages.

Apologetics (pronounced uh-pa-lo-get-iks) is the discipline within religion concerned with defending religious doctrines through systematic reasoning and argument. In other words, it's the study of how to explain, justify, and defend your faith. Here's a breakdown of the concept:

Core Function:

- **Defense of Beliefs:** Apologetics aims to provide a reasoned defense of religious beliefs, addressing challenges and critiques from various perspectives.

Historical Context:

- **Early Christian Apologists:** The term originated with early Christians who defended their faith against persecution and philosophical attacks in the Roman Empire.

Approaches to Apologetics:

There are various approaches apologists take, some emphasizing reason and evidence, while others focus on personal experience or the transformative power of faith. Here are a few common types:

- **Classical Apologetics:** This approach uses logic, philosophy, and evidence (like historical records) to establish the existence of God and the truth claims of a religion.

- **Evidential Apologetics:** This approach focuses on using scientific evidence, historical data, and philosophical arguments to support religious beliefs.

- **Experiential Apologetics:** This approach emphasizes the role of personal experiences and the transformative power of faith in apologetic arguments.

- **Presuppositional Apologetics:** This unique approach argues that non-Christian worldviews are inherently illogical and instead focuses on exposing their inconsistencies.

Goals of Apologetics:

- **Strengthen Faith:** Apologetics can help believers strengthen their own faith by providing a deeper understanding of the reasons behind their beliefs.

- **Address Challenges:** It equips believers to address questions and doubts, along with critiques of their faith from outside perspectives.

- **Promote Faith:** Apologetics can be a tool for promoting faith to others by presenting a reasoned and persuasive case for religious belief.

Importance of Apologetics:

In a world with diverse belief systems and increasing secularism, apologetics can be a valuable tool for those who want to thoughtfully defend and explain their faith.

A Journey Through Time

A Historical Overview of Apologetics

Apologetics, the intellectual defense of religious beliefs, boasts a rich and fascinating history. Let's embark on a journey through the ages, exploring how different eras and contexts shaped the development of apologetic thought:

1. The Early Church (1st-4th Centuries AD): The Rise of the Apologists

- **Context:** Christianity emerged in a world dominated by Roman paganism and Greek philosophy. Early Christians faced persecution and needed to defend their faith.

- **Key Figures:** Justin Martyr, Tertullian, Origen.

- **Apologetic Strategies:** These early apologists aimed to:

o **Demonstrate the superiority of Christianity:** They argued that Christianity fulfilled Jewish prophecies and offered a more ethical and moral way of life compared to paganism.

o **Reconcile faith with reason:** They used Greek philosophy to explain and defend Christian doctrines, appealing to the intellectual elite of the time.

o **Offer historical evidence:** They pointed to the historical reality of Jesus and the early church as proof of the truth of Christianity.

2. The Middle Ages (5th-15th Centuries AD): Reason and Revelation

- **Context:** Christianity became the dominant religion in Europe. Apologetics focused on defending Christian teachings against challenges from within (heresies) and from external philosophies like Islam.

- **Key Figures:** Anselm of Canterbury, Thomas Aquinas.

- **Apologetic Strategies:** Medieval apologists emphasized the harmony between reason and faith:

  ○ **Faith Seeking Understanding:** They believed that faith could be supported and strengthened by reason and logic. Anselm's famous "ontological argument" for the existence of God exemplifies this approach.

  ○ **Systematic Theology:** Thinkers like Aquinas developed systematic theology, meticulously organizing and defending Christian doctrines using logic and philosophical reasoning.

3. The Reformation and the Enlightenment (16th-18th Centuries AD): Shifting Grounds

- **Context:** The Protestant Reformation challenged the authority of the Catholic Church and emphasized individual interpretation of scripture. The rise of Enlightenment thought emphasized reason and scientific inquiry, posing new challenges to religious belief.

- **Key Figures:** Martin Luther, John Locke.

● **Apologetic Strategies:** Apologetics adapted to these new realities:

○ **Sola Scriptura:** Protestant apologists like Luther emphasized the Bible as the sole source of religious authority, using biblical reasoning to defend their beliefs.

○ **Theistic Proofs:** Philosophers like Locke offered arguments for God's existence based on reason and observation of the natural world. These arguments focused on concepts like design and causality.

4. The Modern Era (19th-21st Centuries AD): New Challenges and Responses

● **Context:** Modern science, secularism, and historical criticism of the Bible presented new challenges to religious belief.

● **Key Figures:** C.S. Lewis, Alvin Plantinga.

● **Apologetic Strategies:** Modern apologists continue to grapple with these challenges:

○ **Fiduciary Faith:** Some thinkers, like Kierkegaard, emphasize faith as a leap of trust, acknowledging the limitations of reason in comprehending the divine.

○ **Evidential Apologetics:** Others, like Plantinga, continue to offer arguments for God's existence based on reason and evidence, addressing challenges from science and philosophy.

○ **Incarnational Apologetics:** This approach focuses on the historical reality of Jesus and the impact of Christianity on human history and culture.

Remember:

● This is a very brief overview. Each era has its own nuances and complexities.

● Apologetics is a multifaceted discipline. Different thinkers have employed various strategies and arguments throughout history.

● The need for apologetics continues today, as religious beliefs are still challenged by various movements and schools of thought.

By understanding the historical development of apologetics, you gain a deeper appreciation for the richness and complexity of religious defense. It allows you to see how different approaches have emerged in response to the ever-changing intellectual and cultural landscape.

Defenders of the Early Faith: A Closer Look at Early Church Apologists

The early church fathers who engaged in apologetics played a crucial role in shaping Christianity. Facing persecution, philosophical challenges, and the need to establish their faith in the Roman world, these apologists laid the groundwork for Christian thought. Here's a deeper dive into some of the key figures:

1. Justin Martyr (c. 100 – c. 165 AD): Philosopher and Defender

- **Background:** A former Roman philosopher who converted to Christianity, Justin believed that faith could be reconciled with reason. He addressed pagan emperors directly, writing apologies that defended Christianity and explained its core beliefs.

- **Key Ideas:**

o **Superiority of Christianity:** Justin argued that Christianity fulfilled the prophecies of the Hebrew Bible and offered a superior moral and ethical system compared to paganism.

o **Logos Theology:** He developed the concept of the Logos, the divine reason that permeates the universe and is ultimately identified with Jesus Christ. This concept bridged the gap between Greek philosophy and Christian belief.

○ **Martyrdom as Witness:** Justin saw his potential martyrdom as a testament to the truth of Christianity. He believed that the willingness to die for one's beliefs was a powerful form of persuasion.

2. Tertullian (c. 155 – c. 220 AD): The Lawyer Turned Apologist

• **Background:** A fiery North African convert, Tertullian was known for his passionate and sometimes polemical writings. He defended Christianity against both pagan critics and heretical Christian groups.

• **Key Ideas:**

○ **Prescription Against Heretics:** Tertullian emphasized the importance of apostolic tradition and the authority of the early church in discerning truth from error. He argued against heretical interpretations of Christianity.

○ **The Soul is Naturally Christian:** He believed that there is an innate human awareness of God, evident in the human conscience. This "testimony of the soul" could serve as a point of connection with non-Christians.

○ **Faith and Reason:** Tertullian's famous statement, "Credo quia absurdum est" ("I believe because it is absurd") highlights his emphasis on faith as a leap beyond the limitations of reason.

3. Origen (c. 185 – c. 254 AD): Scholar and Bridge-Builder

• **Background:** A brilliant scholar from Alexandria, Egypt, Origen is considered one of the most influential theologians of the early church. He sought to reconcile Christian faith with Greek philosophy, particularly Platonism.

● **Key Ideas:**

○ **Allegorical Interpretation of Scripture:** Origen believed that the Bible contained multiple layers of meaning, including a literal and a symbolic level. He used allegorical interpretation to harmonize seemingly contradictory passages and present Christianity as intellectually sophisticated.

○ **Preexistence of Souls:** Influenced by Plato, Origen proposed the concept of the preexistence of souls. This idea suggested that souls existed before entering the human body and that salvation involved a return to their original state.

○ **Universal Salvation:** Origen believed that God's love was ultimately redemptive and that all creation, including even the devil, would eventually be reconciled to God. This view was later deemed heretical.

These early church apologists, despite their differences in style and approach, all played a vital role in laying the foundation for Christian thought. Their arguments and writings continue to be studied and debated today.

Further Exploration:

If you'd like to delve deeper, here are some resources:

1. **Primary Sources:** Read excerpts from the writings of Justin Martyr, Tertullian, and Origen in English translation.
2. **Secondary Sources:** Explore scholarly works on the history of early Christian apologetics. Look for books or articles on specific figures or themes mentioned above.

Defending the Faith in the Middle Ages: A Look at Medieval Apologetics

The Middle Ages (roughly 5th to 15th centuries AD) saw a distinct shift in the focus of apologetics compared to the early church. While early apologists primarily defended Christianity against paganism and established its legitimacy, medieval apologists faced a different set of challenges:

- **Internal threats:** Heretical Christian sects like the Cathars challenged core doctrines of the Catholic Church.

- **External threats:** The rise of Islam presented a new religious competitor with its own set of beliefs.

- **Reconciling faith and reason:** Philosophers like Aristotle gained prominence, prompting theologians to reconcile Christian faith with these emerging philosophical ideas.

Here are some key figures and themes that shaped medieval apologetics:

1. The Rise of Systematic Theology:

- **Anselm of Canterbury (1033-1109):** This influential thinker is known for his "ontological argument" for the existence of God. He argued that the very concept of a perfect being (God) necessitates its existence. His work aimed to demonstrate the harmony between faith and reason using logic and philosophical analysis.

- **Peter Lombard (c. 1100-1160):** His book, "Sentences," became a standard theological textbook. It systematized Christian doctrines by compiling and analyzing the writings of church fathers. This approach aimed to present a clear and organized defense of Christian belief.

2. Engaging with Islam:

- **John of Damascus (c. 676-749):** A Syrian Christian theologian living under Muslim rule, John of Damascus wrote extensively in defense of Christianity against Islam. He emphasized the Trinity, the divinity of Christ, and the authority of the Church as key differences between the two faiths.

3. The Influence of Aristotle:

- **Thomas Aquinas (1225-1274):** One of the most influential thinkers of all time, Aquinas used Aristotelian philosophy to create a comprehensive theological system. He argued for the existence of God through arguments like the "First Mover" and the "Unmoved Mover," integrating reason with faith. His work, "Summa Theologica," remains a cornerstone of Catholic theology.

Medieval apologetics differed from the early church in several ways:

- **Focus on Systematic Theology:** Medieval thinkers aimed to create a logically organized and comprehensive defense of Christian belief, drawing heavily on philosophical arguments.

● **Engagement with Heretics and Islam:** Apologetics addressed internal and external threats to the established Christian Church.

● **Integration of Reason and Faith:** Thinkers like Aquinas sought to demonstrate the compatibility of Christian faith with reason and logic, using philosophy as a tool for apologetics.

Further Exploration:

1. **Primary Sources:** Read excerpts from the writings of Anselm of Canterbury, Peter Lombard, and Thomas Aquinas (available in English translation).
2. **Secondary Sources:** Explore scholarly works on medieval theology and philosophy. Look for books or articles on specific figures or themes mentioned above.

Modern Apologetics: Navigating Faith in a Complex World

The modern era (19th-21st centuries AD) has presented Christianity with a unique set of challenges. Scientific advancements, secularization, and philosophical movements like atheism have forced apologists to adopt new strategies for defending the faith. Here's a glimpse into the key themes and approaches of modern apologetics:

1. Responding to Science and Criticism of the Bible:

- **Theistic Evolution:** Some Christian apologists, recognizing the overwhelming evidence for evolution, have embraced the concept of theistic evolution. This view holds that God guided the evolutionary process.

- **Historical Criticism of the Bible:** Scholars who apply historical methods to the Bible raise questions about authorship and accuracy. Modern apologists defend the Bible's trustworthiness, emphasizing its historical core or its inspirational value even if not entirely literal.

2. Evidential Apologetics:

- **Arguments from Design:** These arguments point to the complexity and order of the universe as evidence for a designer, God. The influential works of William Paley ("Natural Theology") exemplify this approach.

• **The Fine-Tuning Argument:** This argument suggests that the universe's physical constants are finely tuned for life, implying an intelligent designer.

3. Philosophical Approaches:

• **Fiduciary Faith:** Thinkers like Søren Kierkegaard emphasize faith as a leap of trust, acknowledging the limitations of reason in comprehending the divine. Faith is a personal commitment based on experience and existential yearning.

• **Incarnational Apologetics:** This approach focuses on the historical reality of Jesus and the impact of Christianity on human history and culture. The life and teachings of Jesus are seen as evidence for the truth of Christianity.

4. Engaging with Atheism:

• **The New Atheism:** The rise of prominent atheist thinkers like Richard Dawkins and Christopher Hitchens has sparked renewed debate. Modern apologists address their arguments concerning the problem of evil, the lack of empirical evidence for God, and the perceived incompatibility of science and religion.

Modern apologetics is characterized by:

• **Adapting to Challenges:** Modern apologists grapple with scientific discoveries, historical criticism, and philosophical critiques of religion.

• **Diverse Approaches:** There's no single approach to apologetics. Some emphasize reason and evidence, while others focus on faith as a personal commitment or the historical impact of Christianity.

- **Engaging with Critics:** Modern apologists actively engage with atheism and other critical perspectives on religion.

Further Exploration:

1. **Primary Sources:** Read works by modern apologists like William Lane Craig, Alvin Plantinga, and Richard Swinburne. Explore writings by prominent atheists like Richard Dawkins and Christopher Hitchens for a balanced perspective.
2. **Secondary Sources:** Look for books and articles on modern apologetics, theistic evolution, or the relationship between science and religion.

A Multifaceted Defense: Exploring Different Types of Apologetics

Apologetics, the discipline of defending religious beliefs, encompasses a wide range of strategies and arguments. Here's a breakdown of some of the most common types:

1. Classical Apologetics: This two-step approach lays the groundwork for Christian apologetics:

- **Theistic Philosophy:** First, it establishes the existence of God through philosophical arguments like the cosmological argument (from the existence of the universe) or the teleological argument (from the design in nature).

- **Evidential Apologetics:** Then, it presents historical and textual evidence for the truth of Christianity, focusing on the life and teachings of Jesus, the reliability of the New Testament, and the early church's historical development.

2. Evidential Apologetics (Stand-alone): This approach focuses on presenting evidence for the truth of Christianity, drawing on various disciplines:

- **Historical Apologetics:** Defends the historical accuracy of the Bible and the reliability of the eyewitness accounts of Jesus' life, miracles, and resurrection.

- **Archaeological Apologetics:** Uses archaeological discoveries to corroborate details mentioned in the Bible, adding weight to its historical accuracy.

• **Scientific Apologetics:** Attempts to harmonize scientific discoveries with religious beliefs. Theistic evolution is a prominent example in Christianity.

3. Philosophical Apologetics: This approach uses philosophical reasoning and arguments to defend core religious beliefs:

• **Theistic Arguments:** These arguments aim to prove the existence of God. Examples include the cosmological argument (mentioned above), the ontological argument (existence based on the concept of a perfect being), and the moral argument (existence based on objective moral values).

• **Epistemological Arguments:** These arguments focus on the nature of knowledge and belief, addressing issues like faith vs. reason and the possibility of religious knowledge.

4. Presuppositional Apologetics: This approach takes a more radical stance, arguing that the basic presuppositions of Christianity (God's existence and the Bible's authority) are self-evident and undeniable:

• **Non-Neutrality of Worldviews:** Presuppositionalists believe all worldviews have built-in assumptions. They argue Christianity's presuppositions are most coherent and rationally defensible.

• **Defense by Offense:** Rather than directly proving God's existence, presuppositionalists focus on exposing the inconsistencies of non-Christian worldviews.

5. Experiential Apologetics: This approach emphasizes personal experiences as evidence for the truth of faith:

● **Conversion Testimonies:** Individuals share their stories of encountering God or experiencing a life-changing conversion, highlighting the transformative power of faith.

● **Religious Experience:** Focuses on the subjective experiences of prayer, worship, or a sense of the divine presence as evidence for God's reality.

6. Relational Apologetics: This approach focuses on building relationships and living out one's faith as a form of apologetics:

● **Authentic Christian Life:** Living a Christ-like life marked by love, compassion, and good works attracts others to Christianity and serves as a powerful defense of the faith.

● **Interfaith Dialogue:** Engaging in respectful dialogue with people of other faiths can foster understanding and appreciation, even if complete agreement isn't reached.

Remember:

● These are just some of the major types of apologetics. There's a lot of overlap and variation within these categories.

● The best approach may depend on the audience and the specific challenges being addressed.

● Some apologetic arguments are more widely accepted than others. Critical thinking and discernment are essential when considering these arguments.

By understanding the different types of apologetics, you gain a broader perspective on how religious beliefs are defended and explored.

Classical Apologetics: The Two-Pronged Defense of Faith

Classical apologetics, a cornerstone of Christian defense strategies, employs a two-step approach to establish the truth of Christianity. Developed primarily in the second millennium AD, it has been influential in shaping Christian thought. Here's a closer look at this foundational approach:

Step 1: Theistic Philosophy - Laying the Groundwork

This initial stage aims to prove the existence of God using philosophical arguments. These arguments don't rely on specifically Christian beliefs but appeal to reason and logic accessible to anyone. Here are some prominent examples:

- **Cosmological Argument:** This argument reasons that everything that exists has a cause. The universe itself must have a cause, which is ultimately God, the uncaused first cause.

- **Teleological Argument (Argument from Design):** This argument points to the order, complexity, and purpose evident in nature as evidence for a designer, God. The intricate design of a watch suggests a watchmaker; the universe's design suggests a divine designer.

- **Moral Argument:** This argument suggests that objective moral values exist. These values must have a source, which is ultimately God, the ultimate source of goodness and morality.

Step 2: Evidential Apologetics - Building the Christian Case

Once the existence of God is established, classical apologetics moves on to demonstrate that Christianity is the true religion. This stage relies on evidence specific to Christianity:

- **Historical Apologetics:** Defends the historical accuracy of the Bible, particularly the New Testament accounts of Jesus' life, teachings, miracles, and resurrection. Eyewitness testimonies and the reliability of early Christian writings are emphasized.

- **Internal Consistency of Scripture:** Classical apologetics argues that the Bible, despite being written by multiple authors over a long period, displays remarkable internal consistency, pointing to its divine inspiration.

- **Fulfillment of Prophecy:** This approach highlights prophecies in the Old Testament that are seen as fulfilled by Jesus and the events of the New Testament, suggesting God's authorship of the biblical narrative.

- **The Early Church:** The rapid spread of Christianity despite persecution and the lives of the early Christians are seen as evidence for the truth of the faith.

Strengths of Classical Apologetics:

- **Systematic Approach:** Provides a logical and organized framework for defending Christian beliefs.

- **Accessibility:** Theistic arguments aim to be universally understandable, appealing to reason even for those unfamiliar with Christianity.

- **Integration of Faith and Reason:** Classical apologetics seeks to show that faith is not blind belief but can be supported by rational arguments.

Criticisms of Classical Apologetics:

- **Presuppositions of Reason:** The effectiveness of theistic arguments relies on the audience accepting certain assumptions about logic and the nature of reality.

- **Challenges to Biblical Accuracy:** Modern historical criticism raises questions about the Bible's inerrancy, potentially undermining the evidential arguments.

- **Problem of Evil:** The existence of suffering and evil in the world seems incompatible with the idea of an all-powerful and all-good God.

Classical apologetics remains a significant approach within Christianity, although it has evolved to address contemporary challenges. The core idea of using reason and evidence to defend faith continues to be relevant for many believers.

Further Exploration:

- **Primary Sources:** Read classic works of Christian apologetics, such as "Summa Theologica" by Thomas Aquinas or "Mere Christianity" by C.S. Lewis. These works showcase how classical apologetics has been applied.

- **Secondary Sources:** Explore scholarly works on the history of Christian apologetics and critiques of theistic arguments. This will give you a more balanced perspective on this approach.

Evidential Apologetics: Building the Case for Christianity with Evidence

Evidential apologetics is a specific approach within Christian apologetics that focuses on presenting evidence to support the truth claims of Christianity. Unlike classical apologetics, it doesn't necessarily require establishing the existence of God beforehand. Here's a deeper dive into this strategy:

Core Tenets:

- **Focus on Evidence:** This approach emphasizes presenting historical, archaeological, philosophical, and even scientific data to bolster Christian beliefs.

- **Varied Lines of Evidence:** Evidential apologists draw from various disciplines to construct a cumulative case for Christianity. No single piece of evidence is seen as conclusive, but the combined weight is persuasive.

- **Accessibility:** While some arguments involve complex reasoning, the goal is to present evidence in a clear and understandable way, appealing to a broad audience.

Types of Evidence Used:

- **Historical Apologetics:** Defends the historical accuracy of the New Testament, particularly the eyewitness accounts of Jesus' life, teachings, miracles, and resurrection. The reliability of early Christian writings and archaeological discoveries that corroborate biblical details are emphasized.

- **Philosophical Apologetics:** Certain philosophical arguments, like the Argument from Design (pointing to the complexity of nature as evidence for a designer), can be used to support the idea of an intelligent being behind creation.

- **Internal Consistency of Scripture:** Evidential apologists may highlight the Bible's underlying unity and coherence despite being written by multiple authors across centuries. This can be seen as evidence for its divine inspiration.

- **Fulfillment of Prophecy:** Passages in the Old Testament interpreted as prophecies fulfilled by Jesus and the events of the New Testament are presented as evidence for God's role in history and the Bible's trustworthiness.

Strengths of Evidential Apologetics:

- **Focus on Data:** Provides a tangible approach to faith, appealing to those who value evidence and reason.

- **Multiple Lines of Argument:** The cumulative weight of evidence from various disciplines can be compelling.

- **Engages with Modern Challenges:** This approach can address questions about the historical accuracy of the Bible or the possibility of reconciling science and faith.

Criticisms of Evidential Apologetics:

● **Selection of Evidence:** Critics argue that apologists might cherry-pick evidence that supports their position while neglecting contradictory data.

● **Interpretation of Evidence:** Different interpretations of the same evidence can exist. For example, archaeological discoveries may be seen as supporting or challenging the Bible depending on the perspective.

● **The Problem of Evil:** The existence of suffering and evil in the world remains a challenge for any argument that posits a benevolent and all-powerful God.

Evidential apologetics is a valuable tool for Christians who want to use reason and evidence to explore and defend their faith. However, it's important to acknowledge the limitations of evidence and the role of faith itself.

Further Exploration:

1. **Primary Sources:** Read works by prominent evidential apologists like William Lane Craig, Josh McDowell, or Gary Habermas. These authors showcase how different lines of evidence are used to defend Christianity.
2. **Secondary Sources:** Explore scholarly works that evaluate the strengths and weaknesses of evidential arguments, historical criticism of the Bible, or the relationship between science and religion.

Presuppositional Apologetics: A Different Approach to Defending the Faith

Presuppositional apologetics is a unique approach within Christian apologetics that stands in contrast to classical or evidential approaches. Here's a breakdown of its key ideas:

Core Tenets:

- **Non-Neutrality of Worldviews:** Presuppositionalists believe everyone has a worldview, a set of basic assumptions about reality, morality, and meaning. These assumptions are foundational and influence how we interpret evidence.

- **Christianity's Self-evident Truth:** Presuppositionalists argue that the core tenets of Christianity, like God's existence and the Bible's authority, are self-evident when examined rationally. They don't require external proof.

- **Defense by Offense:** Rather than directly proving God's existence, presuppositionalists focus on exposing the inconsistencies and logical fallacies of non-Christian worldviews. They believe this ultimately leads to Christianity as the only coherent explanation.

Key Ideas in Presuppositional Apologetics:

- **The Law of Non-Contradiction:** This principle states that something cannot be both true and false at the same time. Presuppositionalists use this principle to expose contradictions in non-Christian worldviews.

• **The Tri-Une God:** The concept of the Trinity (one God in three persons) is seen as a foundational truth with logical implications for morality and human existence.

• **Objective Morality:** Presuppositionalists believe in objective moral values grounded in God's character. Non-Christian worldviews, lacking this foundation, are seen as ultimately subjective and relativistic.

Strengths of Presuppositional Apologetics:

• **Challenges Underlying Assumptions:** Forces people to question their foundational beliefs and consider the possibility of God's existence.

• **Focus on Coherence:** Presuppositionalists emphasize the internal consistency of the Christian worldview.

• **Cultural Relevance:** This approach can be effective in a culture skeptical of traditional arguments for God's existence.

Criticisms of Presuppositional Apologetics:

• **Circular Reasoning:** Critics argue that presuppositional apologetics simply assumes the truth of Christianity from the outset.

• **Dismissive of Other Worldviews:** The emphasis on exposing flaws in other belief systems can be seen as disrespectful or dismissive.

- **Difficulty in Reaching Non-Christians:** The complex
reasoning and terminology used might not be accessible to a
broad audience.

Presuppositional apologetics is a controversial yet intriguing
approach. While it may not be for everyone, it offers a unique
perspective on defending the Christian faith.

Experiential Apologetics: Faith Rooted in Personal Encounters

Experiential apologetics emphasizes personal experiences as evidence for the truth of faith. It focuses on the subjective and transformative power of encountering the divine rather than purely objective arguments or historical analysis.

Here are the core aspects of experiential apologetics:

- **Centrality of Personal Experience:** Conversion testimonies, feelings of peace or purpose attributed to God, and a sense of connection to something larger than oneself are central to this approach.

- **Transformative Power of Faith:** Experiential apologists highlight how faith can lead to positive changes in behavior, improved relationships, and a greater sense of well-being.

- **Focus on Relationship with God:** The emphasis is on a personal connection with God, experienced through prayer, worship, or a sense of divine presence.

Key Ideas in Experiential Apologetics:

- **Subjectivity of Experience:** Experiential apologists acknowledge the subjective nature of religious experiences but argue that their transformative power and impact on one's life hold validity.

• **Accessibility:** Anyone can explore faith through personal experience, making this approach particularly appealing to those seeking a more direct connection with the divine.

• **Complementing Other Forms of Apologetics:** Experiential arguments can work alongside classical or evidential apologetics, providing a more holistic defense of faith.

Strengths of Experiential Apologetics:

• **Relatable and Personal:** Sharing personal stories can be a powerful way to connect with others and inspire them to explore faith.

• **Emphasis on Transformation:** The focus on positive life changes resonates with those seeking meaning and purpose.

• **Openness to Exploration:** Experiential apologetics encourages individuals to explore faith through their own experiences.

Criticisms of Experiential Apologetics:

• **Difficulty in Verification:** Personal experiences are subjective and difficult to objectively verify, making them less persuasive for some.

• **Variation in Experiences:** Religious experiences can vary greatly, leading to questions about the universality of such arguments.

• **Potential for Confirmation Bias:** People may interpret experiences in ways that confirm their existing beliefs.

Experiential apologetics offers a valuable perspective on faith, highlighting the role of personal encounters with the divine. While it may not be the sole approach, it can be a powerful tool for those seeking to connect with others and share their faith journey.

Common Challenges to Faith

Here are some of the most common challenges people face when considering or maintaining faith:

1. The Problem of Evil and Suffering:

- This is a persistent challenge. If God is all-loving and all-powerful, why is there so much evil and suffering in the world? This question can be particularly difficult to grapple with in the face of personal tragedy or widespread crises.

2. Issues of Historical Accuracy and Criticism of the Bible:

- Modern historical criticism of the Bible raises questions about the authorship, accuracy, and inerrancy of scripture. This can create doubt about the Bible's reliability as a foundation for faith.

3. The Challenge of Science:

- Scientific advancements can sometimes seem to contradict religious teachings. For example, evolutionary theory can be seen as challenging the idea of a divine creation. Reconciling faith and science is a complex issue.

4. The Rise of Secularism and Skepticism:

- In an increasingly secularized world, religious beliefs are often questioned or dismissed. This can make it difficult to maintain faith, especially for younger generations.

5. Personal Doubts and Questions:

• Everyone experiences periods of doubt or questioning. This is a natural part of the faith journey. However, unresolved doubts can lead to a weakening of faith.

6. Issues Within Religious Institutions:

• Scandals, hypocrisy, and social controversies involving religious organizations can damage people's trust and lead them to question the validity of organized religion.

7. The Challenge of Finding a Meaningful Faith Tradition:

• With a vast array of religious traditions and denominations, some people struggle to find a faith that resonates with their beliefs and values.

8. The Perceived Disconnect Between Faith and Daily Life:

• Some people may feel that faith doesn't translate well into everyday life. They might question the relevance of religion in a modern world.

It's important to remember that these challenges are not new. People have grappled with these questions for centuries. Many resources and different approaches to apologetics (defending faith) have been developed to address them.

The problem of evil and suffering

The problem of evil and suffering is one of the biggest challenges to faith in a loving and all-powerful God. Here's a deeper look at the issue and some of the proposed responses:

The Problem:

- If God is all-powerful (omnipotent) and all-good (omnibenevolent), then why does evil and suffering exist?

- This suffering can be physical (pain, disease, natural disasters) or emotional (loss, grief, trauma).

- The extent of innocent suffering in the world seems incompatible with the idea of a loving God who has the power to prevent it.

Responses to the Problem of Evil:

- **Free Will Defense:** This argues that God grants humans free will, even though it allows for the possibility of evil choices that cause suffering. Without free will, genuine love and morality wouldn't be possible.

- **Greater Good Defense:** This suggests that suffering may be necessary for a greater good that we can't fully comprehend. Perhaps suffering allows for character development, compassion, or appreciation for happiness.

- **Mystery Defense:** This acknowledges that the coexistence of God's goodness and the presence of evil is a mystery beyond human understanding. Our limited perspective prevents us from grasping God's ultimate plan.

● **Soul-Making Theodicy:** This idea, associated with some theologians, proposes that suffering is necessary for spiritual growth and the development of our souls. Challenges and hardships can refine our character and prepare us for eternity.

Criticisms of the Responses:

● **The Free Will Defense:** Critics argue that God could create a world with free will but without the extreme levels of suffering we see. A truly good God would find a way to minimize suffering.

● **The Greater Good Defense:** This explanation can seem vague and lacks clear evidence for how specific instances of suffering contribute to some greater good.

● **The Mystery Defense:** While acknowledging the mystery is intellectually honest, it can feel like an unsatisfying answer to those who are hurting.

● **The Soul-Making Theodicy:** This view can seem to justify unnecessary suffering, especially of innocent people.

The problem of evil and suffering remains a complex issue with no easy answers. People of faith have grappled with this question for centuries, and the debate continues.

Here are some additional points to consider:

1. Different religious traditions offer varying perspectives on the problem of evil.

2. Some people find comfort in their faith even in the midst of suffering.

3. The question of evil and suffering can lead to a deeper exploration of faith and what it means to believe in God.

Scientific challenges to religious beliefs

Scientific advancements can sometimes clash with religious beliefs, creating challenges for people of faith. Here's a look at some of the most common areas of contention:

1. Origins Debate (Creation vs. Evolution):

• **Religious View:** Many religions believe in a divine creation event, with the Earth and all living things created by God in a relatively short timeframe.

• **Scientific View:** The theory of evolution by natural selection, supported by a vast amount of evidence, suggests that life arose through gradual change over millions of years.

Reconciling the Two:

• **Theistic Evolution:** This view accepts evolution as the mechanism God used to create life. God could have set the laws of nature in motion, leading to the diversity of life we see today.

• **Separate Domains:** Some argue that science explains the "how" of creation, while religion explains the "why," focusing on the purpose and meaning behind existence.

2. Age of the Earth:

• **Religious View:** Some literal interpretations of scripture suggest a young Earth, thousands of years old.

● **Scientific View:** Geological evidence overwhelmingly indicates the Earth is billions of years old.

Reconciling the Two:

● **Interpreting Scripture Symbolically:** Some argue that biblical passages about creation shouldn't be taken literally but understood as metaphorical or conveying spiritual truths.

● **Focus on the Message:** The core message of religious texts about creation may be about God's role as the ultimate source and sustainer of life, not the specific details of the process.

3. Miracles and Science:

● **Religious View:** Many religions believe in miraculous events that defy natural laws.

● **Scientific View:** Science relies on the predictability of natural laws. Miracles, by definition, would be inexplicable by current scientific understanding.

Reconciling the Two:

● **Miracles as Rare Events:** Some argue that miracles are incredibly rare occurrences outside the normal cause-and-effect relationships studied by science.

● **Gaps in Scientific Knowledge:** What science can't explain today might be understood in the future. Miracles could be events we don't yet have the scientific framework to comprehend.

It's important to note that not everyone feels these scientific challenges are incompatible with faith. Many scientists are also people of faith, and they have developed various ways to integrate their scientific understanding with their religious beliefs.

Here are some additional points to consider:

- Some religious traditions are more open to accepting scientific discoveries than others.

- The relationship between science and religion is a complex and ongoing discussion.

- New scientific discoveries may lead to a deeper understanding of both the natural world and the divine.

Pluralism and relativism are two interrelated concepts, but they have distinct meanings. Here's a breakdown to understand the difference:

Pluralism:

- **Definition:** Pluralism refers to the existence of multiple viewpoints, beliefs, or practices within a society or group. It acknowledges the diversity of human thought and experience, especially regarding religion, culture, and morality.

- **Key Aspects:**

○ Respect for Diversity: Pluralism encourages tolerance and understanding of different perspectives, even if they differ from one's own.

○ Peaceful Coexistence: The goal is to find ways for people with different beliefs to live together peacefully and productively.

○ Focus on Shared Values: Despite differences, there may be common ground on fundamental values like peace, justice, or human dignity.

Relativism:

● **Definition:** Relativism goes beyond acknowledging the existence of multiple viewpoints. It suggests that the truth or validity of a belief, practice, or moral value is relative to the specific culture or individual holding it.

● **Key Aspects:**

○ No Universal Truth: Relativism denies the existence of objective truth or universal moral standards. What is right or wrong depends on the context and cultural norms.

○ Cultural Determinism: Beliefs and values are seen as shaped entirely by one's cultural background. There's no basis for judging another culture's practices.

○ Challenges Universality: Relativism can make it difficult to advocate for human rights or criticize harmful practices justified by a particular culture.

The Relationship Between Pluralism and Relativism:

● **Connection:** Pluralism is often seen as a necessary foundation for relativism. If we acknowledge a diversity of viewpoints, it seems logical that truth might be relative.

- **Distinction:** However, it's important to distinguish between the two. Pluralism focuses on peaceful coexistence, while relativism makes claims about the nature of truth itself.

- **Possible to Have One Without the Other:** You can appreciate pluralism (respecting diversity) without fully embracing relativism (denying objective truth).

Criticisms of Relativism:

- **Undermines Morality:** If everything is relative, there can be no basis for objective moral judgments. Harmful practices could be justified if they align with a particular culture.

- **Challenges Progress:** Shared moral values are often needed to address global issues like poverty or environmental degradation. Relativism might hinder such efforts.

- **Difficult to Apply Consistently:** Most people intuitively believe in some form of objective truth, like basic human rights. Absolute relativism can be difficult to maintain in practice.

The debate between pluralism and relativism is complex and ongoing. It raises important questions about tolerance, truth, and the possibility of shared values in a diverse world.

The Role of Reason and Faith

The role of reason and faith in human existence has been a topic of debate for centuries. Here's an exploration of the different perspectives on this relationship:

The Tension Between Reason and Faith:

- **Reason:** Refers to the faculty of logic, critical thinking, and using evidence to form beliefs.

- **Faith:** Refers to a belief system or trust in something not necessarily provable through reason alone. It can be based on personal experience, religious teachings, or intuition.

Historically, there have been two main views on the relationship between reason and faith:

- **Conflict Model:** This view sees reason and faith as fundamentally opposed. Some believe that reason can disprove religious claims, while others believe faith requires a suspension of reason.

- **Compartmentalization:** This view suggests that reason and faith occupy separate domains. Reason is used for worldly matters, while faith takes over in matters of religion and spirituality.

Finding Harmony Between Reason and Faith:

- **Integration:** Many people believe that reason and faith can work together. Reason can be used to examine religious teachings and practices, while faith can provide meaning and purpose in life. (Some forms of apologetics, like classical apologetics, exemplify this approach)

• **Complimentarity:** Reason and faith can be seen as complementary ways of knowing. Reason helps us understand the world around us, while faith can provide answers to questions about meaning, purpose, and the ultimate reality.

• **Fides et Ratio (Faith and Reason):** This concept, emphasized by the Catholic Church, sees faith and reason as two roads leading to the same truth. Faith provides a foundation, while reason helps us understand it more deeply.

Finding the Balance:

The balance between reason and faith can be a personal journey. Some may find comfort in a strong emphasis on faith, while others may prioritize a more reasoned approach.

Here are some additional factors to consider:

• **Denomination:** Different religious traditions have varying views on the role of reason and faith.

• **Individual Temperament:** Some people are naturally more analytical, while others are more intuitive. This can influence how they approach faith.

• **Life Experiences:** Personal experiences, like a profound spiritual encounter or a scientific discovery, can shape one's perspective on reason and faith.

Ultimately, the relationship between reason and faith is a complex and personal one. There's no single "right" answer, and the most important thing is to find a balance that works for you.

Relationship between faith and reason

The relationship between faith and reason is a fascinating and complex question that has been pondered by philosophers and theologians for centuries. Here's a summary of the different perspectives on this topic:

The Tension:

On one hand, reason is the ability to think logically, analyze evidence, and form conclusions based on facts. Faith, on the other hand, is the belief in something without necessarily having concrete proof. This inherent difference can lead to a feeling of tension between the two.

Historical Views:

- **Conflict Model:** This view sees reason and faith as fundamentally opposed. Reason is seen as capable of disproving religious claims, while faith requires a suspension of reason.

- **Compartmentalization:** This view suggests reason and faith occupy separate domains. Reason is used for worldly matters, while faith takes over in matters of religion and spirituality.

Finding Harmony:

Many people believe that reason and faith can coexist and even complement each other:

- **Integration:** Reason can be used to examine religious teachings and practices, while faith can provide meaning and purpose in life. (This approach is exemplified by some forms of apologetics, like classical apologetics)

- **Complementarity:** Reason and faith can be seen as different ways of knowing. Reason helps us understand the physical world, while faith can provide answers to questions about meaning, purpose, and the transcendent.

- **Fides et Ratio (Faith and Reason):** This concept, emphasized by the Catholic Church, sees faith and reason as two roads leading to the same truth. Faith provides a foundation, while reason helps us understand it more deeply.

Finding the Balance:

The balance between reason and faith is a personal journey. Some may find comfort in a strong emphasis on faith, while others may prioritize a more reasoned approach. Here are some additional factors that influence this balance:

- **Denomination:** Different religious traditions have varying views on the role of reason and faith.

- **Individual Temperament:** Some people are naturally more analytical, while others are more intuitive. This can influence how they approach faith.

- **Life Experiences:** Personal experiences, like a profound spiritual encounter or a scientific discovery, can shape one's perspective on reason and faith.

Examples:

● **Evidential Apologetics:** This approach uses reason and evidence (like historical records or philosophical arguments) to support the truth claims of Christianity.

● **Experiential Apologetics:** This approach emphasizes the role of personal experiences and the transformative power of faith.

Ultimately, the relationship between reason and faith is a complex and personal one. There's no single "right" answer, and the most important thing is to find a balance that works for you.

Limits of human understanding

The vastness of the universe and the complexities of our own existence present us with inherent limitations in what we can fully understand. Here are some fundamental aspects of these limits:

Cognitive Limits:

- **Brain Complexity:** Our brains, while incredibly sophisticated, have a finite processing capacity. We can only handle a certain amount of information at once, limiting our ability to grasp highly complex concepts.

- **Sensory Perception:** Our senses provide us with a limited view of reality. We can only perceive a narrow range of the electromagnetic spectrum, for instance, and there might be entire dimensions beyond our sensory reach.

- **Language and Symbolism:** We rely on language and symbols to understand the world, but these tools can also be limiting. Language can be imprecise, and symbols may not perfectly capture the essence of reality.

Knowledge Limitations:

- **Incomplete Information:** Our knowledge is constantly evolving, but it's always based on the information we have access to. There's vast amounts of information in the universe we haven't yet discovered.

- **The Problem of Induction:** We often rely on past experiences to make assumptions about the future, but this isn't always reliable. New discoveries can challenge our existing understanding.

- **The Limits of Science:** While science is a powerful tool for understanding the world, it may not be able to answer all our questions. There might be fundamental aspects of reality that lie beyond the scientific method.

Philosophical Limitations:

- **The Mind-Body Problem:** The relationship between our minds and bodies remains a mystery. We don't fully understand how consciousness arises from physical processes.

- **Free Will vs. Determinism:** The question of whether we have free will or if our choices are predetermined is a complex one that we may never have a definitive answer to.

- **The Nature of Reality:** What is real? Is there an objective reality out there, or is our experience of the world entirely subjective? These are profound questions that philosophers have grappled with for centuries.

The Limits Don't Negate the Journey:

While these limitations exist, they don't negate the human drive to explore, understand, and make sense of the world around us. The very act of acknowledging these limits can fuel our curiosity and inspire us to keep learning and searching for answers.

Here are some additional points to consider:

- The concept of limits can be subjective. What one person finds incomprehensible, another might be able to grasp to a certain extent.

• Technological advancements can push the boundaries of human understanding. New tools and methods of observation can help us perceive the universe in ways we never imagined before.

• The limitations can be a source of wonder and awe. The vastness of the unknown can inspire a sense of humility and a deeper appreciation for the mysteries of existence.

Even though we may never have all the answers, the pursuit of understanding itself is a valuable human endeavor. The limitations of human understanding are what drive our continued exploration and the progress of knowledge throughout history.

Developing an Apologetic Mindset

Here's a roadmap to develop an apologetic mindset, which equips you to defend your beliefs and engage in thoughtful discussions about faith:

1. Solidify Your Own Foundation:

- **Know Your Beliefs:** Start by clearly understanding your own religious beliefs and the core tenets of your faith tradition. What are the foundational truths you hold dear?

- **Explore Sacred Texts:** Immerse yourself in your religion's scripture or core texts. Careful study can deepen your understanding and provide resources for apologetic arguments.

- **Grasp Historical Context:** Understanding the historical and cultural context in which your religious texts were written can provide valuable insights for interpreting them.

2. Learn About Different Approaches to Apologetics:

- **Classical Apologetics:** Explore the two-pronged approach of establishing God's existence and then the truth claims of Christianity (or your religion) through reason and evidence.

- **Evidential Apologetics:** Learn how this approach uses various types of evidence (historical, philosophical, scientific) to support religious beliefs.

• **Experiential Apologetics:** Consider the role of personal experiences and the transformative power of faith in apologetic arguments.

• **Presuppositional Apologetics:** Understand this unique approach that focuses on exposing the inconsistencies of non-Christian worldviews rather than directly proving God's existence.

3. Engage with Friendly Critics:

• **Discuss with Fellow Believers:** Talk to knowledgeable people within your faith tradition. Discuss apologetic arguments, explore challenging questions, and learn from each other.

• **Seek Mentorship:** Find a mentor or religious leader who can guide you in developing your apologetic skills and answer your questions.

• **Read Works by Apologists:** Explore writings by prominent apologists within your tradition. This will expose you to different approaches and arguments.

4. Broaden Your Knowledge Base:

• **Philosophy:** A basic understanding of philosophy, especially logic and epistemology (the study of knowledge), can be helpful in constructing sound apologetic arguments.

• **Science:** While science can sometimes challenge religious beliefs, a basic understanding of scientific concepts can help you navigate these discussions.

● **World Religions:** Learning about other belief systems can broaden your perspective and equip you to better understand and respond to their claims.

5. Develop Your Communication Skills:

● **Clear and Concise Communication:** Be able to articulate your beliefs clearly and concisely, avoiding jargon or overly complex explanations.

● **Respectful Dialogue:** Remember that the goal is to have a thoughtful conversation, not to win an argument. Be respectful of others' viewpoints.

● **Active Listening:** Listen attentively to understand the other person's perspective before responding. This fosters genuine dialogue.

Developing an apologetic mindset is a continuous process. It involves self-reflection, learning, and practice. By cultivating a strong foundation in your own beliefs, exploring different apologetic approaches, and refining your communication skills, you can effectively engage in conversations about faith.
Additional Tips:

● **Be Honest About What You Don't Know:** It's okay to admit you don't have all the answers. This honesty can build trust and open the door for further exploration.

● **Focus on Shared Values:** Even amidst differing beliefs, there might be common ground on fundamental values like compassion, justice, or peace. Highlight these shared values.

● **Live Your Faith:** Ultimately, the best apologetic is how you live your life. Let your actions demonstrate the positive impact your faith has on you and the world around you.

Remember, apologetics is not about forcing your beliefs on others. It's about thoughtfully engaging with questions about faith, respectfully defending your position, and ultimately pointing others towards a deeper truth you believe in.

Cultivating intellectual humility

Cultivating intellectual humility is a journey of self-awareness and a commitment to lifelong learning. Here are some steps you can take to embrace this valuable mindset:

Recognize Your Limitations:

- **Accept you don't have all the answers:** No one does! Acknowledge that your knowledge and understanding are constantly evolving.

- **Be aware of biases:** We all have biases shaped by our upbringing, experiences, and culture. Be mindful of how these biases might influence your thinking.

- **Embrace the Dunning-Kruger Effect:** This cognitive bias suggests that people with limited knowledge tend to overestimate their competence. The more you learn, the more you realize how much you don't know.

Embrace a Growth Mindset:

- **See challenges as opportunities:** View setbacks and uncertainties as opportunities to learn and grow intellectually.

- **Welcome feedback:** Don't shy away from constructive criticism. See it as a chance to refine your understanding and identify areas for improvement.

- **Be open to new ideas:** Don't be afraid to question your own assumptions and consider alternative perspectives.

Practice Active Learning:

- **Ask thoughtful questions:** Don't be afraid to ask questions, even if they seem basic. Curiosity is the fuel for intellectual growth.

- **Seek out diverse viewpoints:** Read books and articles by people with different perspectives. Engage in respectful conversations with those who hold different beliefs.

- **Step outside your comfort zone:** Challenge yourself by learning about unfamiliar topics or disciplines.

Focus on Understanding:

- **Listen actively:** Pay close attention to what others are saying, try to understand their perspective, and avoid interrupting.

- **Seek clarification:** If something is unclear, don't hesitate to ask for clarification or rephrasing.

- **Focus on the merits of the argument:** Evaluate arguments based on their logic and evidence, not who is presenting them.

Benefits of Intellectual Humility:

- **Improved decision-making:** By acknowledging your limitations and considering various perspectives, you can make more informed decisions.

● **Stronger relationships:** Intellectual humility fosters open communication and fosters mutual respect in your interactions with others.

● **Lifelong learning:** A humble approach keeps you open to new information and ideas, enriching your life with continuous learning.

Remember, cultivating intellectual humility is an ongoing process. Be patient with yourself, celebrate your progress, and enjoy the journey of lifelong learning!

Here are some additional tips:

● **Practice self-reflection:** Regularly reflect on your thinking patterns, biases, and areas where you might need to learn more.

● **Celebrate intellectual curiosity:** Embrace the joy of learning and discovery for its own sake.

● **Be a role model:** Demonstrate intellectual humility in your interactions with others, encouraging open and respectful dialogue.

By embracing intellectual humility, you open yourself up to a world of possibilities, fostering deeper understanding, stronger relationships, and a richer perspective on life.

The importance of listening and empathy

Listening and empathy are fundamental human skills that are crucial for building strong relationships, fostering connection, and navigating complex situations. Here's why they're so important:

The Power of Listening:

- **Understanding Others:** True listening goes beyond simply hearing words. It involves paying attention to nonverbal cues, emotions, and the underlying message the speaker is trying to convey.

- **Validating Feelings:** When you listen attentively, you acknowledge the speaker's emotions and experiences, making them feel heard and understood.

- **Building Trust:** By being a good listener, you demonstrate respect and care for the other person. This builds trust and strengthens relationships.

- **Gathering Information:** Effective listening allows you to gather all the necessary information before responding. This is essential for resolving conflicts or making sound decisions.

The Role of Empathy:

- **Stepping into Another's Shoes:** Empathy is the ability to understand and share the feelings of another person. It involves seeing the world from their perspective.

● **Compassion and Connection:** Empathy fosters compassion, the urge to help and support others. It also creates a deeper connection between people.

● **Conflict Resolution:** By understanding the other person's perspective, you can approach disagreements with more empathy and find solutions that work for everyone.

● **Improved Communication:** Empathy allows you to communicate more effectively, tailoring your message to resonate with the listener's feelings and experiences.

Why Listening and Empathy Matter:
In today's fast-paced world, we often prioritize talking over listening. However, strong listening and empathy skills are essential for:

● **Healthy Relationships:** Both personal and professional relationships thrive on mutual understanding and respect, which stem from good listening and empathy.

● **Effective Teamwork:** Collaboration and problem-solving require listening to different perspectives and working together towards a common goal.

● **Quality Customer Service:** Understanding customer needs and concerns is key to providing excellent service.

● **Social and Emotional Learning (SEL):** These skills are important for children to develop healthy relationships, manage emotions, and resolve conflicts peacefully.

How to Improve Listening and Empathy:

- **Practice Active Listening:** Pay attention, make eye contact, and avoid interrupting. Ask clarifying questions and summarize what you've heard to ensure understanding.

- **Be Patient:** Give the speaker your full attention and time to express themselves completely.

- **Recognize Nonverbal Cues:** Pay attention to body language, facial expressions, and tone of voice to understand the full message.

- **Reflect and Respond:** Take a moment to process what you've heard before responding. Show empathy by acknowledging the speaker's feelings.

By actively developing your listening and empathy skills, you can create stronger connections with others, build trust, and navigate the complexities of life with greater understanding and compassion.

Continuous learning and growth

Continuous learning and growth are essential for a fulfilling life in today's ever-changing world. Here's a breakdown of the benefits and how to cultivate this mindset:

Benefits of Continuous Learning:

- **Staying Relevant:** The world is constantly evolving, and new knowledge and skills are needed to thrive in various aspects of life, both personal and professional.

- **Enhanced Skills and Knowledge:** Continuous learning allows you to develop and refine your existing skills, as well as acquire new ones. This can open doors to new opportunities.

- **Improved Problem-Solving:** By expanding your knowledge base and exploring different perspectives, you become better equipped to tackle challenges and find creative solutions.

- **Boosted Confidence:** Learning new things and mastering skills gives you a sense of accomplishment and boosts your confidence in your abilities.

- **Increased Creativity:** Exposure to new ideas and information sparks creativity and innovation, allowing you to approach situations from fresh angles.

- **Mental Stimulation:** Continuous learning keeps your mind sharp and engaged, potentially reducing the risk of cognitive decline as you age.

- **Greater Personal Satisfaction:** Learning and growth can be a source of deep personal satisfaction and fulfillment. It allows you to explore your interests and passions.

Cultivating a Growth Mindset:

- **Embrace Challenges:** View challenges and setbacks as opportunities to learn and grow. Don't be discouraged by mistakes; see them as stepping stones on your learning journey.

- **Develop Curiosity:** Foster a genuine curiosity about the world around you. Ask questions, explore new topics, and be open to new experiences.

- **Set Goals:** Having specific learning goals can provide direction and motivation. These goals can be short-term or long-term, personal or professional.

- **Find a Learning Style:** Discover how you learn best. Do you prefer reading, watching videos, attending workshops, or hands-on experiences?

- **Celebrate Milestones:** Acknowledge and celebrate your progress, no matter how small. This will help you stay motivated and keep moving forward.

- **Seek Out Mentors and Role Models:** Surround yourself with people who inspire you to learn and grow. Learn from their experiences and successes.

- **Make Learning Enjoyable:** Find ways to make learning enjoyable. Explore topics you're genuinely interested in, and experiment with different learning methods.

Continuous learning can be a lifelong adventure. By embracing a growth mindset, setting goals, and finding ways to make learning enjoyable, you can unlock a world of possibilities and keep growing as a person.

Here are some additional tips:

- **Dedicate Time to Learning:** Schedule specific times for learning in your daily or weekly routine.

- **Utilize Available Resources:** There are countless resources available online and in libraries to support your learning goals.

- **Embrace Different Learning Formats:** Explore online courses, podcasts, audiobooks, documentaries, and workshops to keep things interesting.

- **Share Your Knowledge:** Teaching what you learn to others is a powerful way to solidify your understanding and make learning a social experience.

Remember, continuous learning is not about achieving perfection. It's about enjoying the journey of exploration, expanding your horizons, and becoming the best version of yourself.

1. Key Scriptural Support for Apologetics

1.1 1 Peter 3:15 - The Cornerstone of Christian Apologetics

"But in your hearts revere Christ as Lord. Always be prepared to give an answer to everyone who asks you to give the reason for the hope that you have. But do this with gentleness and respect."

This verse serves as the primary biblical mandate for apologetics. Let's break it down:

- "In your hearts revere Christ as Lord": This prefaces the call to apologetics with a reminder of the believer's primary allegiance. Effective apologetics flows from a heart devoted to Christ.

- "Always be prepared": This implies ongoing study and reflection. Apologetics isn't just for experts but for all believers.

- "To give an answer": The Greek word used here is "apologia," from which we derive "apologetics." It suggests a reasoned defense, not just an emotional response.

- "To everyone who asks you": Apologetics is presented as a responsive activity. We're called to engage with those who inquire, not to force our views on the unwilling.

- "The reason for the hope that you have": Our apologetic should focus on the core of our faith - the hope we have in Christ.

- "With gentleness and respect": The manner of our apologetic is as important as its content. We're called to engage with humility and consideration for others.

1.2 Jude 3 - The Call to Contend for the Faith

"Dear friends, although I was very eager to write to you about the salvation we share, I felt compelled to write and urge you to contend for the faith that was once for all entrusted to God's holy people."

This verse introduces a more active, even combative, aspect of apologetics:

- "Contend for the faith": The Greek word used here, "epagonizomai," suggests an intense struggle or fight. It implies that defending the faith may sometimes involve rigorous debate or confrontation with opposing views.

- "Once for all entrusted": This phrase emphasizes the unchanging nature of the core Christian message. Apologetics isn't about creating new doctrines but defending established truths.

1.3 Colossians 4:6 - The Character of Apologetic Discourse

"Let your conversation be always full of grace, seasoned with salt, so that you may know how to answer everyone."

This verse provides guidance on the nature of apologetic conversations:

- "Full of grace": Our apologetics should reflect the grace we've received in Christ.

- "Seasoned with salt": In ancient times, salt was used as a preservative and to add flavor. Our arguments should be both enduring and engaging.

- "Know how to answer everyone": This suggests tailoring our approach to each individual, recognizing that different people may need different types of explanations or evidence.

1. Biblical Examples of Apologetics

2.1 Old Testament Examples

a) Moses before Pharaoh (Exodus 5-12) Moses' interactions with Pharaoh serve as an early example of apologetics in action. He presented evidence of God's power through signs and wonders, arguing for the reality of the Hebrew God against the backdrop of Egyptian polytheism. This narrative demonstrates how apologetics can involve not just verbal arguments but also demonstrations of divine power.

b) Elijah on Mount Carmel (1 Kings 18:20-40) Elijah's contest with the prophets of Baal is a dramatic example of apologetics. He publicly challenged the prevailing religious beliefs, setting up a demonstrable test to prove the power of the true God. This episode illustrates how apologetics can sometimes involve public confrontations and empirical demonstrations.

c) Daniel in Babylon (Daniel 1-6) Daniel's life in Babylon provides multiple examples of defending and demonstrating the faith in a hostile cultural environment. His wisdom, integrity, and miraculous experiences served as powerful apologetic tools in a pagan court.

2.2 New Testament Examples

a) Jesus' Apologetic Methods Jesus frequently engaged in apologetic discourse:

- Responding to challenges about the Sabbath (Mark 2:23-28): Jesus used logical arguments and scriptural interpretation to defend His actions.

- Answering questions about His authority (Matthew 21:23-27): He employed strategic questioning to expose the motives and inconsistencies of His critics.

- Addressing doubts about His resurrection (Luke 24:36-43): Jesus provided empirical evidence to support His bodily resurrection.

b) Paul's Apologetic Ministry The Apostle Paul was perhaps the most prolific apologist in the early church:

● Reasoning in the synagogues (Acts 17:2-3): Paul used scriptural exegesis to argue for Jesus as the Messiah.

● Speech at the Areopagus (Acts 17:22-34): This famous discourse demonstrates contextual apologetics, as Paul engaged with Greek philosophical ideas to present the gospel.

● Defense before Agrippa (Acts 26:1-29): Paul's legal defense doubled as a presentation of the gospel, showcasing how apologetics can be integrated into various life situations.

1. Theological Implications of Biblical Apologetics

The biblical basis for apologetics carries several important theological implications:

3.1 The Rationality of Faith By calling believers to provide reasons for their hope, Scripture affirms that faith is not blind or irrational. It suggests that belief in God can withstand intellectual scrutiny and rational inquiry.

3.2 The Importance of Intellectual Engagement The biblical emphasis on being prepared to answer questions implies that intellectual engagement with our faith is not optional but an essential part of Christian discipleship.

3.3 The Interplay of Divine Revelation and Human Reason Biblical apologetics often involves a combination of appealing to divine revelation (Scripture) and employing human reason. This suggests a complementary relationship between faith and reason in Christian thought.

3.4 The Universal Relevance of the Gospel The call to be ready to answer "everyone" implies that the Christian message is universally relevant and can be meaningfully communicated across cultural and intellectual boundaries.

3.5 The Ethical Dimension of Apologetics The repeated emphasis on gentleness, respect, and grace in apologetic encounters underscores that the manner of our defense is as important as its content. This aligns with the broader biblical ethic of love and respect for all people.

Conclusion

The biblical basis for apologetics is robust and multifaceted. From explicit commands to implicit examples, Scripture consistently portrays faith as something to be explained, defended, and shared with others in a thoughtful manner. This biblical foundation not only justifies the practice of apologetics but also provides guidance on how it should be conducted. As we move forward in our study of apologetics, this scriptural basis will serve as a touchstone, informing both the content of our arguments and the spirit in which we present them.

The Importance of Apologetics in the Modern World

In an era marked by rapid technological advancement, cultural shifts, and increasingly diverse worldviews, the practice of Christian apologetics has taken on renewed significance. This section explores the multifaceted importance of apologetics in navigating the complex landscape of modern society.

1. Addressing Intellectual Challenges to Faith

1.1 Scientific Advancements The ongoing dialogue between science and religion continues to shape public discourse. Apologetics plays a crucial role in:

- Addressing perceived conflicts between scientific discoveries and biblical accounts

• Demonstrating the compatibility of faith with scientific inquiry

• Exploring the limitations of scientific methodology in answering existential questions

1.2 Philosophical Objections Modern and postmodern philosophical perspectives often challenge traditional religious beliefs. Apologetics helps in:

• Engaging with arguments from atheism, agnosticism, and skepticism

• Addressing the problem of evil and suffering from a Christian perspective

• Exploring questions of meaning, purpose, and morality in a secular age

1. Navigating Religious Pluralism

2.1 Interfaith Dialogue In an increasingly interconnected world, Christians frequently encounter adherents of other faiths. Apologetics is vital for:

• Articulating the unique claims of Christianity in a multi-faith context

• Fostering respectful and meaningful interfaith conversations

• Addressing misconceptions about Christianity held by other religious groups

2.2 Responding to Relativism The prevalence of moral and religious relativism in modern society poses challenges to absolute truth claims. Apologetics aids in:

- Defending the concept of objective truth in a "post-truth" culture
- Articulating a coherent Christian worldview amidst competing ideologies
- Addressing the claim that all religions are essentially the same

1. Engaging with Digital Culture

3.1 Information Overload The internet age has made vast amounts of information readily available. Apologetics is crucial for:

- Helping believers navigate conflicting information about faith
- Equipping Christians to discern credible sources from misinformation
- Providing accessible, well-reasoned responses to common objections found online

3.2 Social Media Discourse The rise of social media has changed the nature of public discourse. Apologetics is important for:

- Engaging in constructive dialogues about faith in digital spaces
- Countering viral misinformation or misrepresentations of Christianity

- Modeling respectful and thoughtful communication in polarized online environments

1. Addressing Cultural Shifts

4.1 Changing Moral Landscapes Rapid changes in societal norms and values often challenge traditional Christian ethics. Apologetics helps in:

- Articulating a Christian perspective on controversial social issues

- Defending the relevance and wisdom of biblical morality in contemporary contexts

- Engaging with critiques of Christian ethics from secular humanist perspectives

4.2 Postmodern Influences Postmodern thought has influenced how many people approach truth claims. Apologetics is vital for:

- Addressing skepticism towards metanarratives, including the Christian gospel

- Engaging with subjective approaches to truth and morality

- Demonstrating the coherence and explanatory power of the Christian worldview

1. Strengthening the Faith of Believers

5.1 Doubt and Deconstruction Many Christians, especially younger generations, grapple with doubt and faith deconstruction. Apologetics serves to:

- Provide intellectual support for faith during periods of questioning
- Offer robust responses to common doubts and objections
- Demonstrate that faith can withstand rigorous intellectual scrutiny

5.2 Deepening Understanding Apologetics encourages a deeper engagement with Christian doctrine and practice:

- Fostering a more mature and reflective faith

- Encouraging critical thinking and intellectual curiosity within a faith context

- Bridging the gap between academic theology and everyday Christian life

1. Equipping for Evangelism

6.1 Removing Intellectual Barriers For many, intellectual objections are obstacles to considering the Christian faith. Apologetics helps in:

- Addressing common misconceptions that prevent openness to the gospel
- Demonstrating the reasonableness of Christian beliefs to skeptics
- Providing evidence-based arguments that complement personal testimony

6.2 Contextualizing the Gospel Effective evangelism in the modern world often requires tailoring the presentation of the gospel to specific cultural contexts. Apologetics aids in:

- Identifying key issues and questions relevant to different demographics

- Translating Christian concepts into language accessible to various worldviews

- Demonstrating the relevance of Christian faith to contemporary life

Conclusion

The importance of apologetics in the modern world cannot be overstated. As Christians navigate an increasingly complex and often challenging cultural landscape, apologetics provides essential tools for understanding, articulating, and defending the faith. It serves not only to address external challenges but also to deepen the believer's own understanding and conviction.

Moreover, apologetics plays a crucial role in bridging the gap between faith and reason, demonstrating that Christianity is not merely a set of private beliefs but a comprehensive worldview capable of engaging with the most pressing questions of our time. In an age of information, misinformation, and competing ideologies, the practice of apologetics equips believers to confidently and compassionately present the hope they have in Christ, fulfilling the biblical mandate to always be prepared to give an answer.

As we move forward in our exploration of apologetics, this understanding of its contemporary importance will inform our approach, helping us to develop strategies that are both faithful to Christian tradition and relevant to the modern context.

The Importance of Apologetics in the Modern World

1. Addressing Intellectual Challenges to Faith

In the 21st century, Christianity faces a myriad of intellectual challenges that were largely unforeseen by previous generations. The rapid advancement of human knowledge across various disciplines has led to questions and criticisms that demand thoughtful, well-reasoned responses from believers. Apologetics plays a crucial role in addressing these challenges, providing a robust intellectual framework that supports faith in an increasingly skeptical world.

1.1 Scientific Advancements

The relationship between faith and science has been a topic of intense debate for centuries, but recent scientific discoveries have brought this discussion to the forefront of public consciousness. Apologetics is essential in navigating this complex terrain, helping believers and skeptics alike understand the compatibility of Christian faith with scientific inquiry.

One of the primary areas where apologetics intersects with science is in discussions about origins. The theory of evolution, Big Bang cosmology, and discoveries in genetics have all raised questions about the biblical account of creation. Apologists engage with these scientific theories, often demonstrating that they need not conflict with a Christian worldview. For instance, many apologists argue for various interpretations of Genesis that allow for an old earth and evolutionary processes, while still maintaining the core Christian belief in God as the ultimate creator.

Moreover, apologetics addresses the common misconception that science and faith are inherently at odds. By highlighting the contributions of Christian scientists throughout history and pointing out the philosophical assumptions underlying scientific inquiry, apologists demonstrate that faith and science can be complementary rather than contradictory. They often argue that the orderliness and intelligibility of the universe, which make scientific investigation possible, align well with the Christian concept of a rational Creator.

Another crucial role of apologetics in relation to scientific advancements is in exploring the limitations of scientific methodology. While science is incredibly powerful in explaining natural phenomena, it operates within certain boundaries. Apologetics helps to articulate questions that lie beyond the scope of scientific inquiry – questions of purpose, meaning, and morality. By doing so, it demonstrates the continued relevance of faith in a scientifically advanced world.

Apologetics also engages with specific scientific theories that seem to challenge traditional Christian beliefs. For example, neuroscientific research on consciousness and decision-making has raised questions about free will, a concept central to Christian theology. Apologists work to reconcile these scientific findings with Christian teachings, often drawing on philosophical arguments about the nature of consciousness and moral responsibility.

Furthermore, apologetics addresses the use (and sometimes misuse) of scientific authority in public discourse. In an age where "science says" is often invoked as the final word on any subject, apologists help to foster critical thinking. They encourage both believers and skeptics to examine the actual evidence behind scientific claims, to understand the difference between established facts and theoretical interpretations, and to recognize when scientific authority is being extended beyond its proper domain.

In engaging with scientific advancements, Christian apologetics does not aim to discredit or deny scientific findings. Instead, it seeks to demonstrate that Christian faith can integrate scientific knowledge into a coherent worldview. This approach not only strengthens the faith of believers who may struggle with apparent conflicts between science and religion but also presents a more nuanced and intellectually satisfying version of Christianity to skeptics who may have dismissed faith as incompatible with scientific thinking.

[This section would continue with more detailed discussions of specific scientific advancements and how apologetics engages with them, providing examples, counterarguments, and the implications for Christian faith and practice.]

1.2 Philosophical Objections

In addition to scientific challenges, Christianity faces numerous philosophical objections in the modern world. These objections often strike at the core of Christian beliefs, questioning the very foundations of faith. Apologetics plays a vital role in addressing these philosophical challenges, providing reasoned responses that demonstrate the intellectual credibility of Christian thought.

One of the most persistent philosophical objections to Christianity is the problem of evil and suffering. This age-old question asks how an all-powerful, all-knowing, and all-loving God can allow evil and suffering to exist in the world. The importance of apologetics in addressing this issue cannot be overstated, as it touches both the intellectual and emotional aspects of faith.

Apologists approach the problem of evil from various angles. Some, like Alvin Plantinga, have developed sophisticated logical arguments, such as the free will defense, which posits that a world with free beings who can choose to do good or evil is more valuable than a world of automatons. Others, like C.S. Lewis in "The Problem of Pain," explore the potential redemptive purposes of suffering. Still others, like N.T. Wright, emphasize the Christian narrative of God entering into human suffering through Jesus Christ.

By engaging with the problem of evil, apologetics not only provides intellectual responses but also offers pastoral care to those grappling with personal experiences of suffering. It helps believers maintain faith in difficult times and presents a thoughtful Christian perspective to skeptics who see suffering as evidence against God's existence.

Another significant philosophical challenge addressed by apologetics is the question of God's existence itself. In an increasingly secular world, arguments for atheism and agnosticism have gained prominence. Apologetics responds to these challenges by reviving and refining classical arguments for God's existence, such as the cosmological, teleological, and moral arguments.

For instance, the Kalam Cosmological Argument, popularized by philosopher William Lane Craig, argues for a first cause of the universe based on scientific evidence for the Big Bang. The Fine-Tuning Argument points to the precise calibration of universal constants as evidence for a designer. Moral arguments, advanced by thinkers like C.S. Lewis and more recently Ravi Zacharias, contend that the existence of objective moral values points to a transcendent source of morality.

These philosophical arguments serve not only to defend the rationality of belief in God but also to challenge the assumptions of naturalism and materialism that often underlie atheistic worldviews. By doing so, apologetics helps to level the intellectual playing field, demonstrating that theism is a rationally viable option in the marketplace of ideas.

Apologetics also engages with postmodern philosophical objections to Christianity. In a cultural context where absolute truth claims are viewed with suspicion, Christian apologists must navigate complex discussions about the nature of truth, knowledge, and interpretation. They often draw on the work of philosophers like Alvin Plantinga and his concept of "warranted Christian belief" to argue that Christian faith can be rationally justified even in a postmodern context.

Moreover, apologetics addresses philosophical challenges to specific Christian doctrines. For example, the concept of the Trinity or the incarnation of Christ often faces objections on logical grounds. Apologists work to demonstrate the internal coherence of these doctrines, drawing on rich theological traditions and contemporary philosophical tools to articulate these beliefs in ways that are intellectually satisfying.

The field of apologetics also engages with questions of meaning and purpose that arise in existentialist and nihilist philosophies. In a world where many find traditional sources of meaning eroded, Christian apologetics offers a robust alternative. It argues that Christianity provides a coherent framework for understanding human existence, offering purpose, value, and hope in the face of apparent cosmic indifference.

By addressing these philosophical objections, apologetics serves several crucial functions. It strengthens the faith of believers by providing intellectual support for their beliefs, equipping them to engage confidently with challenging ideas. It also presents Christianity as an intellectually rigorous option to seekers and skeptics, demonstrating that faith and reason are not mutually exclusive.

Furthermore, apologetics contributes to broader philosophical discussions, ensuring that Christian perspectives are represented in academic and public discourse. This engagement helps to counteract stereotypes of Christianity as anti-intellectual or reliant solely on blind faith.

[The chapter would continue to explore other philosophical objections and the apologetic responses to them, discussing the implications for Christian faith and practice in the modern world.]

2. Navigating Religious Pluralism

In our increasingly interconnected world, Christianity no longer exists in isolation but stands alongside a multitude of religious and spiritual beliefs. This religious pluralism presents both challenges and opportunities for Christian faith, making apologetics more crucial than ever.

2.1 Interfaith Dialogue

Interfaith dialogue has become an essential aspect of religious discourse in the modern world. Christians frequently encounter adherents of other faiths in their daily lives, workplaces, and communities. Apologetics plays a vital role in equipping believers to engage in these interactions thoughtfully and respectfully.

One of the primary challenges in interfaith dialogue is articulating the unique claims of Christianity without appearing exclusivist or intolerant. Apologists help Christians navigate this delicate balance by providing frameworks for discussing distinctive Christian doctrines, such as the Trinity or the incarnation, in ways that are clear and respectful.

For instance, when discussing the Christian belief in Jesus as the unique Son of God with Muslims, apologists might draw on shared concepts of monotheism while carefully explaining the Christian understanding of the Trinity. They might explore the Islamic view of Jesus as a prophet, using it as a starting point to discuss the Christian belief in His divinity.

Apologetics also aids in addressing common misconceptions about Christianity held by other religious groups. For example, many Hindus might view Christianity as just another path to the same ultimate reality. Apologists help Christians explain the exclusive claims of Christ in a way that acknowledges the sincerity of other beliefs while maintaining the integrity of Christian doctrine.

Moreover, apologetics equips Christians to engage with the philosophical and ethical teachings of other religions. By fostering a deep understanding of Christian theology and ethics, apologetics enables believers to enter into meaningful comparisons and contrasts with other worldviews. This approach not only enhances mutual understanding but also sharpens Christians' grasp of their own faith.

Importantly, apologetics in interfaith contexts is not about "winning" arguments but about fostering mutual understanding and respectful dialogue. It involves not only speaking but also listening, seeking to understand other perspectives while clearly articulating one's own beliefs.

2.2 Responding to Relativism

Religious pluralism often gives rise to relativistic attitudes towards truth claims. The notion that "all religions are essentially the same" or that "all paths lead to God" has gained popularity in many circles. Apologetics plays a crucial role in addressing these relativistic views while maintaining a respectful stance towards other beliefs.

Apologists often begin by pointing out the logical inconsistencies in religious relativism. They might demonstrate how different religions make mutually exclusive truth claims that cannot all be simultaneously true. For instance, the Christian belief in a personal God who became incarnate in Jesus Christ is fundamentally different from the Buddhist concept of non-theistic enlightenment.

At the same time, apologetics seeks to affirm the common ground that exists between different faiths without compromising on essential Christian doctrines. This might involve acknowledging shared ethical values or similar historical roots while clearly articulating where Christianity diverges from other belief systems.

Apologetics also addresses the philosophical underpinnings of relativism itself. It challenges the assumption that all truth is subjective or culturally determined, arguing instead for the existence of objective truth. This often involves engaging with postmodern philosophies and demonstrating how the Christian worldview offers a coherent alternative to relativistic thinking.

Furthermore, apologetics helps Christians respond to the charge of arrogance often leveled at those who maintain exclusive truth claims. Apologists argue that believing in objective truth doesn't necessarily equate to close-mindedness or intolerance. They might point out that it's possible to hold firm convictions while still respecting and engaging with those who hold different views.

In addressing relativism, apologetics also tackles the question of religious pluralism in relation to salvation. The exclusive claims of Christianity regarding salvation through Christ alone can be challenging to articulate in a pluralistic context. Apologists help believers navigate this terrain, often drawing on biblical exegesis and theological reflection to explain the Christian understanding of salvation while maintaining a humble and compassionate stance.

Ultimately, the goal of apologetics in responding to relativism is not to denigrate other beliefs but to demonstrate the coherence and plausibility of the Christian worldview. It seeks to show that Christianity offers a robust framework for understanding reality that can stand up to intellectual scrutiny while addressing the deepest longings of the human heart.

[The chapter would continue to explore other aspects of navigating religious pluralism, such as the challenges posed by secularism and the rise of "spiritual but not religious" attitudes, always emphasizing the role of apologetics in helping Christians engage thoughtfully with these issues.]

3. Engaging with Digital Culture

In the 21st century, the digital revolution has fundamentally altered the landscape of human interaction, information dissemination, and belief formation. This shift presents unique challenges and opportunities for Christian apologetics, making it more crucial than ever in the modern world.

3.1 Information Overload

The internet age has ushered in an era of unprecedented access to information. While this has many benefits, it also presents significant challenges for Christian faith and apologetics.

One of the primary issues is the sheer volume of information available. Internet users are bombarded with a constant stream of data, opinions, and arguments, many of which challenge Christian beliefs. Apologetics plays a vital role in helping believers navigate this information deluge.

For instance, a simple online search about the historical Jesus can yield results ranging from serious scholarly work to fringe conspiracy theories, all presented with seeming authority. Apologetics equips Christians with the tools to discern credible sources from misinformation. This involves not only providing sound arguments for Christian beliefs but also teaching critical thinking skills.

Apologists often emphasize the importance of evaluating sources, understanding the difference between peer-reviewed academic work and popular opinion, and recognizing logical fallacies. They might provide guidelines for assessing the credibility of online information, such as checking author credentials, looking for citations, and cross-referencing with reputable sources.

Moreover, apologetics addresses the challenge of information silos and echo chambers that often form in digital spaces. In an age where algorithms curate personalized content, it's easy for believers to become isolated from challenging viewpoints. Apologetics encourages engagement with diverse perspectives, helping Christians understand and respond to the best arguments against their faith rather than only encountering weak caricatures.

Another crucial role of apologetics in the digital age is providing accessible, well-reasoned responses to common objections found online. Many people, especially younger generations, turn to the internet as their first source of information about religion. Apologetics ensures that thoughtful Christian perspectives are available amidst the sea of online content.

This might involve creating engaging digital content — videos, podcasts, infographics — that present apologetic arguments in formats suited to digital consumption. It also means being present on various online platforms, from social media to forums, to engage in discussions and provide reasoned responses to questions and objections.

3.2 Social Media Discourse

Social media has become a primary arena for public discourse, including discussions about faith and religion. This presents both opportunities and challenges for Christian apologetics.

One of the main challenges is the often polarized and combative nature of social media debates. The anonymity and distance provided by digital platforms can lead to heated exchanges that generate more heat than light. Apologetics in this context involves not only presenting sound arguments but also modeling respectful and constructive dialogue.

Apologists often emphasize the importance of digital civility, encouraging Christians to engage in online discussions with grace and patience. They might provide strategies for de-escalating tense interactions, finding common ground with those who disagree, and presenting Christian perspectives in ways that invite dialogue rather than defensiveness.

Another challenge is the rapid spread of misinformation and misrepresentations of Christianity on social media. Memes, out-of-context quotes, and sensationalized headlines can quickly go viral, shaping public perceptions of Christian beliefs. Apologetics plays a crucial role in countering these distortions by providing accurate information and thoughtful responses.

This might involve creating shareable content that succinctly addresses common misconceptions, or training Christians to recognize and respond to viral misinformation about their faith. Apologists might also engage directly with high-profile critics of Christianity on social media platforms, modeling respectful but robust defense of the faith in public forums.

The brevity encouraged by many social media platforms presents another challenge. Complex theological concepts or historical arguments often don't lend themselves to 280-character tweets or short video clips. Apologetics in this context involves the skill of distilling complex ideas into concise, engaging formats without oversimplifying or misrepresenting the issues.

At the same time, social media offers unprecedented opportunities for apologetics to reach wide audiences. Apologists can now engage in real-time with people from diverse backgrounds and beliefs, spanning geographical and cultural boundaries. This allows for a more dynamic and responsive form of apologetics, addressing questions and challenges as they arise in the public consciousness.

Furthermore, social media provides platforms for building communities of learning and support around apologetics. Online groups, live streaming events, and interactive Q&A sessions allow believers to engage with apologetic content and receive support in their own faith journeys.

In all these digital engagements, the goal of apologetics remains the same as in face-to-face interactions: to present the Christian faith as reasonable and compelling, to address objections with grace and truth, and to invite others into a deeper exploration of Christian beliefs.

3.2 Social Media Discourse (continued)

Helping believers navigate conflicting faith information
In the vast landscape of social media, Christians often encounter conflicting information about their faith. This can range from different interpretations of scripture to outright contradictions of core beliefs. Apologetics plays a crucial role in helping believers navigate this confusing terrain.

Apologists often provide frameworks for evaluating conflicting information. This might include:

1. Encouraging believers to return to primary sources, particularly the Bible, rather than relying solely on secondary interpretations.
2. Teaching the importance of context in understanding both scriptural passages and historical Christian teachings.
3. Providing resources that explain and defend orthodox Christian positions on controversial topics.
4. Helping believers understand the historical development of Christian doctrine, which can clarify why certain interpretations are considered orthodox and others heretical.

Moreover, apologetics in this context often involves fostering critical thinking skills among believers. This includes teaching logical reasoning, identifying fallacies, and understanding the difference between strong and weak arguments, regardless of whether they support or challenge one's existing beliefs.

Equipping Christians to discern credible sources

In an era where anyone can publish content online, discerning credible sources of information about faith has become a crucial skill.

Apologetics plays a vital role in equipping Christians with the tools to evaluate the reliability of online sources.

Apologists might provide guidelines such as:

1. Checking the credentials and background of authors or speakers
2. Looking for citations and references to reputable scholarly works
3. Being wary of sensationalist claims or headlines
4. Crosschecking information with recognized Christian leaders and institutions
5. Understanding the difference between peer-reviewed academic work and popular opinion pieces

Furthermore, apologetics in this area often involves teaching Christians about the various branches of theology, biblical scholarship, and church history. This knowledge helps believers contextualize the information they encounter and better assess its credibility.

Providing accessible responses to common online objections

The internet has amplified the voices of critics of Christianity, making their objections more widely accessible than ever before. Apologetics serves a crucial function in providing equally accessible responses to these common online objections.

This often involves:

1. Creating easily shareable content (infographics, short videos, memes) that address common misconceptions or criticisms of Christianity.
2. Developing comprehensive yet understandable responses to complex objections, breaking down philosophical or theological concepts into layman's terms.
3. Maintaining active presences on popular social media platforms to engage directly with doubts and questions as

they arise.

4. Collaborating with Christian influencers and content creators to reach wider audiences with apologetic content.

5. Providing resources that help believers articulate responses to objections in their own words, rather than just memorizing stock answers.

Apologists also recognize the importance of tone in these online interactions. They often model and teach how to respond to objections with patience, respect, and intellectual honesty, even in the face of hostile or mocking criticisms.

By focusing on these aspects, apologetics helps create a more informed, discerning, and articulate Christian presence in online spaces. This not only strengthens the faith of individual believers but also presents a more thoughtful and engaging face of Christianity to the broader online world.

# 4. Addressing Cultural Shifts

The modern world is characterized by rapid and significant cultural changes that often challenge traditional Christian beliefs and practices. Apologetics plays a crucial role in helping Christians navigate these shifts while maintaining the integrity of their faith.

4.1 Changing Moral Landscapes

One of the most prominent areas where cultural shifts have created challenges for Christianity is in the realm of ethics and morality. The modern world has seen dramatic changes in societal norms and values, particularly in areas such as sexuality, gender roles, and the sanctity of life.

Apologetics in this context involves articulating a Christian perspective on controversial social issues in a way that is both faithful to biblical teachings and engaging with contemporary concerns. This is a delicate balance, requiring both firmness in conviction and sensitivity to the complexities of human experience.

For instance, on the issue of same-sex relationships, apologists must navigate between affirming the traditional Christian sexual ethic and responding compassionately to the lived experiences of LGBTQ+ individuals. This might involve explaining the biblical basis for traditional views on marriage while also addressing accusations of bigotry or outdated thinking. Apologists often emphasize the Christian call to love all people while maintaining that love doesn't necessarily mean affirming all choices or lifestyles.

Another significant area is the ongoing debate around abortion and the sanctity of life. Apologetics in this realm involves not only presenting biblical and philosophical arguments for the pro-life position but also engaging with complex social and ethical questions about women's rights, healthcare access, and support for mothers and children.

Apologists also address emerging ethical issues related to technological advancements, such as genetic engineering, artificial intelligence, and transhumanism. These developments raise profound questions about the nature of humanity and the limits of scientific intervention in human life. Christian apologetics seeks to bring biblical wisdom and theological reflection to bear on these cutting-edge ethical dilemmas.

In all these discussions, apologetics aims to demonstrate the continued relevance and wisdom of Christian ethics in contemporary contexts. This often involves showing how Christian moral teachings are not arbitrary rules but are grounded in a holistic understanding of human flourishing and the nature of reality.

Moreover, apologetics addresses the common critique that Christian morality is outdated or oppressive. Apologists might argue that Christian ethics, properly understood, promote human dignity, social justice, and the common good. They often point to the historical contributions of Christianity to human rights, education, and social welfare as evidence of the positive impact of Christian values on society.

4.2 Postmodern Influences

Postmodern thought has significantly influenced contemporary culture, challenging many of the assumptions that underlie traditional Christian apologetics. This shift requires a nuanced apologetic approach that engages with postmodern critiques while still affirming the truth claims of Christianity.

One of the key challenges posed by postmodernism is skepticism towards metanarratives or grand explanatory stories about reality. Christianity, with its overarching narrative of creation, fall, redemption, and restoration, is often viewed with suspicion in postmodern contexts. Apologetics in this environment involves demonstrating the coherence and explanatory power of the Christian worldview without falling into the trap of intellectual imperialism.

Apologists might engage with postmodern thought by acknowledging the limitations of human knowledge and the influence of cultural context on our understanding, while still arguing for the existence of objective truth. They might draw on the work of philosophers like Alvin Plantinga to argue that belief in God can be "properly basic" - rationally held without needing to be proved by argument.

Another significant postmodern influence is the emphasis on subjective experience and personal narrative. While this can pose challenges to traditional apologetic approaches that focus on logical arguments and historical evidence, it also presents opportunities. Apologists can engage with this aspect of postmodern thought by emphasizing the experiential dimension of Christian faith, sharing personal testimonies, and exploring how the Christian narrative gives meaning to individual life stories.

The postmodern critique of power structures and hidden agendas also impacts apologetics. Christianity, particularly in its institutional forms, is often viewed as a tool of oppression or social control. Apologetics in this context involves addressing these critiques head-on, acknowledging historical failures of the church while also highlighting Christianity's role in promoting human rights, social justice, and individual liberation.

Furthermore, postmodern influences have led to increased emphasis on diversity and pluralism, challenging the exclusive truth claims of Christianity. Apologetics in this context involves articulating Christian beliefs in ways that acknowledge the value of diverse perspectives while still maintaining the uniqueness of Christ. This might involve exploring concepts like "inclusive exclusivism" that affirm the universal scope of God's love while maintaining the centrality of Christ in salvation.

In all these engagements with postmodern thought, the goal of apologetics is not to simply refute postmodernism but to show how Christianity can engage meaningfully with postmodern insights while offering a more satisfying and coherent worldview. This approach recognizes that many aspects of postmodern thought - such as skepticism towards totalizing systems and sensitivity to marginalized voices - can actually enrich Christian thinking and practice.

[The chapter would continue to explore other cultural shifts, such as the rise of neo-paganism, the influence of Eastern spiritualities in the West, and the challenges posed by consumerism and materialism to Christian values.]

5. Strengthening the Faith of Believers

In an era of increasing skepticism and challenges to faith, apologetics plays a crucial role in strengthening the convictions of believers. This aspect of apologetics is not just about defending against external criticisms but also about nurturing a deeper, more resilient faith within the Christian community.

A. Addressing Common Doubts

1. Reconciling faith and science:

The perceived conflict between faith and science has been a stumbling block for many believers. This chapter aims to bridge this gap by exploring how faith and science can coexist and even complement each other.

We'll start by examining the historical context of this perceived conflict, tracing its roots to events like the Galileo affair and the Scopes trial. It's crucial to understand that many early scientists were people of faith who saw their work as uncovering the wonders of God's creation.

Next, we'll address specific areas where faith and science are often seen to be in conflict:

a) Creation and evolution: We'll explore various perspectives within the faith community, from young-earth creationism to theistic evolution. The goal is not to prescribe a single view but to show how different believers have reconciled their faith with scientific evidence.

b) The age of the universe: We'll discuss how some interpret the "days" in Genesis metaphorically and how this aligns with current scientific understanding.

c) Miracles and natural law: We'll examine how miracles can be understood within a scientific worldview, considering them as rare events that don't negate the overall consistency of natural laws.

We'll then highlight examples of harmony between faith and science:

• The Big Bang theory, proposed by Georges Lemaître, a Catholic priest and physicist, aligns with the concept of a universe with a beginning.

• The fine-tuning of universal constants, which some see as evidence of design.

• The way scientific discoveries can deepen our appreciation of creation's complexity and beauty.

We'll also discuss the limitations of both science and religion:

• Science can describe how the natural world works but can't answer questions of purpose or meaning.

• Religion addresses existential and moral questions that are beyond the scope of scientific inquiry.

Finally, we'll provide practical advice for believers struggling with this issue:

• Encourage ongoing education in both faith and science.

• Promote dialogue between scientists and theologians.

• Emphasize that faith can provide a framework for interpreting scientific discoveries without contradicting them.

1. Dealing with the problem of evil and suffering:

This section will tackle one of the most challenging issues for many believers: how can a good and all-powerful God allow evil and suffering in the world?

We'll begin by clearly stating the problem, often formulated as: If God is all-powerful, all-knowing, and all-good, why does evil exist? We'll explore various theodicies (defenses of God's goodness in view of evil) proposed throughout history.

Key points to cover include:

a) Free will defense: Evil exists because God gave humans free will, which allows for the possibility of choosing evil.

b) Soul-making theodicy: Suffering can lead to personal growth and character development.

c) Natural law theodicy: Many instances of suffering result from the consistent operation of natural laws, which are necessary for a stable, inhabitable universe.

d) Eschatological theodicy: The belief that all suffering will be redeemed or compensated for in an afterlife.

We'll also address specific challenging scenarios, such as:

- Natural disasters and their impact on innocent people
- The suffering of children
- The existence of seemingly gratuitous evil

The section will include philosophical and theological perspectives, but also practical and pastoral approaches to dealing with suffering. We'll discuss:

- The importance of empathy and compassion in responding to others' suffering

- How faith communities can provide support during times of hardship

- Personal testimonies of those who have found their faith strengthened through suffering

1. Understanding apparent contradictions in religious texts:

This part will address the concern many believers have when they encounter passages in their sacred texts that seem to contradict each other or conflict with modern ethical standards.

We'll start by acknowledging that these apparent contradictions exist and that it's normal and even beneficial to wrestle with them. The goal is not to provide a definitive answer for every difficulty, but to offer approaches for understanding and reconciling them.

Key points to cover:

a) Hermeneutics: We'll discuss principles of interpretation, including the importance of considering historical and cultural context, literary genre, and the overall message of the text.

b) Progressive revelation: The idea that God's revelation to humanity has been gradual and progressive, adapting to human understanding over time.

c) Allegorical and metaphorical interpretations: How some apparent contradictions can be resolved by understanding certain passages as non-literal.

d) Textual criticism: An introduction to how scholars study ancient manuscripts to understand the original text and its meaning.

We'll examine specific examples of apparent contradictions and difficult passages, such as:

- Differing accounts of events in the Gospels
- Old Testament laws that seem harsh by modern standards
- Passages that appear to conflict with scientific understanding

The section will also address:

- The role of faith traditions and religious authorities in interpreting texts

- How to approach personal Bible study when encountering difficult passages

- The value of engaging with diverse perspectives and scholarly resources

Throughout this section, we'll emphasize that wrestling with these issues can lead to a deeper, more nuanced faith. We'll encourage readers to approach apparent contradictions as opportunities for growth and deeper understanding rather than as threats to their faith.

B. Deepening Theological Understanding: A Journey into the Heart of Faith

Have you ever felt a yearning to go beyond the basic tenets of your faith? Perhaps you've encountered questions about the "why" and "how" behind your religious beliefs. This section is your guide on a thrilling exploration – a quest to truly understand the core of your faith tradition. We'll delve into three key areas that will enrich your understanding and deepen your connection to your religion.

1. Unveiling the Core: A Deep Dive into Doctrines

Every religion rests on foundational beliefs called doctrines. These are the essential truths that define the faith and guide its practices. Imagine them as the pillars upon which your religion is built. Let's explore how to truly understand these doctrines:

- **Meaning and Significance:** Each doctrine has a rich meaning that unfolds layer by layer. Start by examining the core message it conveys. What does it teach you about God, humanity, and the world? How does it connect to other doctrines within your faith?

- **Scriptural Basis:** Doctrines don't exist in a vacuum. They are grounded in the sacred texts of your religion. Explore the specific passages that inform each doctrine. Analyze the language used and how it contributes to the overall understanding.

- **Historical Context:** Remember, doctrines weren't formed in a bubble. Understanding the historical context in which they emerged is crucial. Were there specific events, controversies, or philosophical currents that influenced their development? Seeing doctrines through this historical lens allows for a more nuanced appreciation.

- **Real-World Application:** Doctrines aren't just abstract ideas. They have a profound impact on how believers live their lives. Explore how each core belief translates into practical actions. How does it guide ethical decision-making? What specific practices or rituals are rooted in these doctrines?

2. A Journey Through Time: Studying the Historical Development of Beliefs

Our faith traditions haven't always been static. Doctrines have evolved and adapted over time. Let's embark on a historical journey to understand this fascinating process:

- **Tracing the Roots:** Where did your faith's core doctrines originate? Who were the key figures involved in their development? What were the initial interpretations and how did they evolve?

- **Shifting Sands:** Doctrines haven't always been set in stone. Throughout history, there have been debates, controversies, and even schisms related to their interpretation. Explore these pivotal moments. What were the central arguments? How did these debates ultimately shape the current understanding of the doctrines?

- **The Influence of Context:** Doctrines don't develop in isolation. Social, political, and philosophical movements of the time all play a role. Analyze how these external factors influenced the way believers interpreted their core beliefs. For example, did scientific advancements challenge existing doctrines, leading to new interpretations?

3. A Tapestry of Interpretations: Examining Diverse Theological Perspectives

Your faith tradition is likely not monolithic. Within it, there may be various schools of thought or denominations with slightly different takes on core doctrines. Let's explore this rich tapestry of interpretations:

- **Schools of Thought:** Delve into the different theological perspectives that exist within your faith. What are the key differences in their interpretations of core doctrines? How do these variations influence rituals, practices, and the overall understanding of the religion?

- **Engaging with Difference:** Look beyond the boundaries of your own tradition. How do other faiths or denominations approach similar theological concepts? What insights can be gained from studying these comparative perspectives? This can broaden your understanding and challenge your own assumptions.

- **Modern Challenges:** The world is constantly changing, and our faith traditions need to adapt. Explore how contemporary issues like scientific advancements or social changes challenge traditional interpretations of doctrines. How are theologians within your faith grappling with these new realities? Are there new interpretations emerging to address these challenges?

C. Cultivating Spiritual Disciplines: Nurturing the Seed of Faith

Faith is a seed with the potential to blossom into a vibrant and life-enriching experience. But just like any plant, it requires regular care and nourishment. This section explores the essential spiritual disciplines that will help you cultivate your faith and deepen your connection to the divine.

1. The Power of Prayer: A Direct Line to the Divine

Prayer is the cornerstone of most spiritual traditions. It's a form of communication, a way to express your gratitude, voice your concerns, and seek guidance from a higher power. Here's why prayer is so important:

- **Connection and Relationship:** Prayer fosters a sense of connection with the divine. It allows you to express your love, devotion, and dependence on a higher power. Regular prayer strengthens this relationship, fostering a sense of security and comfort.

- **Transformation and Growth:** Prayer can be a powerful tool for personal transformation. By expressing your vulnerabilities and desires in prayer, you open yourself to guidance and growth. Prayer can also be a source of strength and solace during difficult times.

- **Manifestation and Gratitude:** Prayer can be a way to express your desires and petitions to the divine. While it doesn't guarantee specific outcomes, the act of focusing on your hopes and expressing gratitude for blessings received can be transformative.

2. Meditation: Quieting the Mind to Hear the Divine Voice

Meditation is the practice of quieting the mind and focusing your attention. It's a way to cultivate inner peace, gain clarity, and connect with something deeper than yourself. Here's how meditation can enhance your spiritual life:

- **Inner Peace and Stillness:** In our fast-paced world, meditation offers a precious space for stillness and inner peace. By quieting the constant mental chatter, you create space to connect with your inner self and the divine presence within you.

- **Heightened Awareness:** Meditation sharpens your focus and awareness. It allows you to become more mindful of your thoughts, emotions, and the world around you. This heightened awareness can deepen your appreciation for the beauty and wonder of existence.

- **Guidance and Inspiration:** Meditation can be a gateway to receiving guidance and inspiration from the divine. By calming the mind, you create space for insights, intuition, and a deeper understanding of your spiritual path.

3. The Strength of Community: Worship and Service

Spiritual growth is rarely a solitary journey. Being part of a faith community provides support, encouragement, and a sense of belonging. Here are two key aspects of community involvement:

- **Shared Worship:** Participating in communal worship rituals connects you to something larger than yourself. Singing hymns, chanting prayers, or engaging in other sacred practices fosters a sense of unity and shared purpose. These rituals can also be deeply moving and inspire a sense of awe and wonder.

● **Service to Others:** An essential aspect of most spiritual traditions is service to others. Helping those in need allows you to connect with your faith on a practical level. It fosters compassion, humility, and a sense of interconnectedness with all beings.

By incorporating these spiritual disciplines into your life, you'll be nurturing the seed of faith and allowing it to blossom into a vibrant and enriching experience. Remember, consistency is key. The more you cultivate these practices, the deeper your connection to the divine will become.

D. Responding to Cultural Challenges: Living Your Faith in a Complex World

Modern life can sometimes feel like a constant negotiation between your faith and the broader cultural landscape. This section equips you with tools to navigate these complexities and confidently live your faith in a changing world.

1. Thriving in a Secular World: Finding Faith in Unexpected Places

Many societies today are becoming increasingly secular. This doesn't mean your faith has to become irrelevant. Here are some ways to find meaning and purpose in a secular environment:

- **Living by Example:** Your actions speak louder than words. Let your core values – kindness, compassion, integrity – radiate through your interactions with others. This can be a powerful way to showcase the positive impact of your faith.

- **Finding Common Ground:** Focus on shared values you hold with those from different backgrounds. Compassion, justice, and helping others in need are values often shared across cultures and religions. Building bridges through these commonalities can foster understanding and respect.

- **Creating Your Sacred Space:** Even in a secular environment, you can carve out sacred spaces for your faith practices. This could be a designated prayer corner in your home, attending religious services online, or finding quiet moments for meditation amidst your busy schedule.

2. Navigating Moral Dilemmas: Applying Faith to Contemporary Issues

The world throws a lot of moral dilemmas our way. Advances in technology, social changes, and complex ethical questions can challenge your faith. Here's how your faith can guide you:

- **Seeking Guidance from Scripture:** Look to your religion's sacred texts for wisdom on ethical issues. Many religious traditions offer timeless principles that can be applied to contemporary situations.

- **Engaging with Religious Leaders:** Seek guidance from trusted religious leaders within your community. They can provide insights from their own experiences and interpretations of your faith's teachings.

- **Forming Your Moral Compass:** Use your faith's core values to develop your own internal moral compass. Reflect on how these values would guide you in navigating specific ethical dilemmas. Remember, there may not always be easy answers, but your faith can provide a framework for making thoughtful decisions.

3. Embracing Interfaith Dialogue: Respectful Engagement with Other Worldviews

Our world is beautifully diverse, with a multitude of faiths and beliefs. Here's how to approach this diversity with respect:

- **Open-Mindedness and Curiosity:** Approach other religions with an open mind and a genuine curiosity. Seek to understand their core beliefs and practices. This can foster empathy and appreciation for the richness of human experience.

- **Finding Common Ground:** As mentioned earlier, focus on shared values. Look for areas where your faith and others overlap, such as promoting peace, social justice, or environmental stewardship. Building bridges through these commonalities can foster interfaith cooperation.

- **Respectful Disagreements:** There will inevitably be differences in beliefs. Learn to disagree respectfully. Engaging in civil dialogue allows for mutual understanding and growth, even if complete agreement isn't reached.

By embracing these approaches, you can navigate cultural challenges with confidence and grace. Remember, living your faith in a complex world doesn't mean isolating yourself. It's about finding ways to connect with others, share your values, and contribute to a more peaceful and harmonious world.

E. Personal Testimonies and Experiences: The Power of Faith in Our Lives

Faith is a deeply personal journey. It's about how our beliefs shape our experiences, offering solace, strength, and a sense of purpose. This section delves into the power of faith through personal testimonies – stories of individuals transformed by their beliefs.

1. Seeds of Faith Taking Root: Stories of Transformation

- **From Lost to Found:** Include stories of people who found meaning and direction through their faith. Perhaps they overcame addiction, found peace after a loss, or experienced a profound shift in perspective. These narratives showcase the transformative power of faith.

- **Unexpected Paths:** Not all faith journeys are linear. Share stories of people who questioned their beliefs, encountered challenges, or explored different religious paths before finding their true connection. These narratives highlight the authenticity and complexity of personal faith journeys.

2. Finding Meaning and Purpose: Faith as a Guiding Light

- **A Compass in Chaos:** Explore how faith provides a sense of meaning and purpose in the face of life's challenges. Share stories of individuals who drew strength from their beliefs to navigate difficult times, overcome obstacles, or find hope in the midst of despair.

- **Living with Intention:** Faith can inspire us to live with intention and purpose. Include narratives of people who use their faith to guide their actions, make ethical decisions, or contribute positively to their communities. These stories showcase how faith translates into meaningful action.

3. Divine Intervention: Experiences of Guidance and Grace

- **Moments of Clarity:** Some people describe feeling a divine presence intervening in their lives, offering guidance or support during critical moments. Include stories where individuals received unexpected help, a sudden surge of strength, or a feeling of inner peace that they attribute to their faith. These narratives acknowledge the role of the divine in personal experiences.

- **Answered Prayers:** Many people find comfort and strength in the belief that their prayers are heard. Share stories where individuals prayed for specific outcomes and experienced a positive resolution, which they attribute to the power of prayer. These narratives acknowledge the importance of prayer in personal faith.

Remember:

- Emphasize the diversity of experiences. Include stories from people of different backgrounds, ages, and denominations.

- Focus on the transformative impact. Showcase how faith has made a positive difference in people's lives.

- Maintain a respectful tone. While personal experiences are powerful, avoid making claims of religious superiority or criticizing other belief systems.

By incorporating these elements, you can create a compelling section that celebrates the power of faith in the lives of ordinary people. These stories can inspire readers to reflect on their own journeys and connect with the universal themes of hope, purpose, and the divine.

F. Apologetics as a Tool for Personal Growth: Defending Your Faith While Deepening Your Understanding

Apologetics, often referred to as "defending the faith," might seem confrontational. But at its core, it's a powerful tool for personal growth. Here's how studying apologetics can strengthen your own faith journey:

1. Sharpening Your Critical Thinking Skills

Apologetics equips you to analyze information critically. You'll learn to:

- **Distinguish Fact from Opinion:** Apologetics trains you to evaluate the evidence behind claims, both for and against your faith. This skill is valuable in all aspects of life, not just religious discussions.

- **Identify Logical Fallacies:** Deceptive arguments often masquerade as logical reasoning. Apologetics teaches you to recognize these fallacies, protecting you from manipulation and strengthening your ability to think clearly.

- **Ask Tough Questions:** A strong faith can handle honest inquiry. Apologetics encourages you to grapple with challenging questions about your beliefs, leading to a more nuanced and defensible understanding.

2. Mastering the Art of Articulation

Apologetics helps you communicate your faith effectively. You'll learn to:

- **Articulate Your Beliefs Clearly:** Being able to explain your core beliefs in a clear and concise way is essential. Apologetics provides the tools to articulate your faith with confidence, even to those unfamiliar with your religion.

- **Navigate Difficult Conversations:** Religious discussions can get heated. Apologetics teaches you to approach these conversations respectfully, focusing on understanding and finding common ground.

- **Bridge the Communication Gap:** Many objections to faith stem from misunderstandings. Apologetics equips you to explain complex theological concepts in a way that is clear, engaging, and respectful of your audience.

3. Building Confidence in Your Faith

By engaging with apologetics, you gain a deeper understanding of your own beliefs. This fosters a sense of confidence and security in your faith:

- **Understanding the "Why" Behind Your Beliefs:** Apologetics encourages you to explore the historical, philosophical, and theological foundations of your faith. This deeper understanding strengthens your convictions and allows you to speak with authority about your beliefs.

- **Addressing Doubts and Challenges:** Everyone experiences moments of doubt. Apologetics equips you with the knowledge and tools to address these doubts and find answers to challenging questions. This intellectual engagement can solidify your faith.

- **Becoming a Well-Informed Believer:** Apologetics empowers you to move beyond blind faith. By studying the evidence and arguments surrounding your beliefs, you become a more informed and confident believer.

Remember:

• Apologetics is a tool for personal growth, not just religious debates.

• The goal is to understand your own faith better and communicate it effectively, not to win arguments.

• Approach discussions with respect and a genuine desire for understanding, even when you disagree.

By using apologetics as a tool for personal exploration and growth, you can deepen your faith, strengthen your convictions, and confidently share your beliefs with the world.

G. Building a Resilient Faith: Weathering the Storms of Life

Faith is not a fragile flower that wilts at the first sign of adversity. A truly resilient faith can withstand life's challenges, emerging stronger and more meaningful. This section explores how to cultivate a faith that can weather any storm.

1. Doubt as a Stepping Stone, Not a Stumbling Block

Doubt is a natural part of the faith journey. Many wrestle with questions, inconsistencies, or challenges to their beliefs. Here's why doubt can actually be a positive force:

- **A Catalyst for Deeper Understanding:** Doubt can propel you to delve deeper into your faith, seeking answers to your questions. This exploration can lead to a more nuanced and personal understanding of your beliefs.

- **Strengthening Your Convictions:** When you grapple with doubts and emerge with your faith intact, your convictions become stronger. This process builds resilience and makes your faith more authentic.

- **Openness to Growth:** Doubt can be a sign of an open mind. It allows you to consider different perspectives and integrate them into your evolving faith journey.

2. Forging a Faith that Endures: Facing Challenges with Confidence

Life throws curveballs. Here's how your faith can be a source of strength during difficult times:

- **A Source of Hope and Comfort:** Faith can offer solace in the face of loss, suffering, or uncertainty. Knowing you are not alone and that you have a higher power to guide you can provide comfort and strength.

- **A Framework for Meaning Making:** Faith can help you find meaning in difficult experiences. It can offer a perspective that transcends immediate suffering and allows you to see the bigger picture.

- **A Community of Support:** Many faith traditions offer a strong sense of community. Knowing you have a network of people to support you through challenges can be a tremendous source of strength.

3. The Dance of Certainty and Humility: Finding Balance
A healthy faith embraces both certainty and humility:

- **Holding Core Beliefs with Conviction:** There are core tenets of your faith that provide a foundation and stability. It's important to hold these beliefs with conviction, allowing them to guide your actions and decisions.

- **Acknowledging the Limits of Knowledge:** No one has all the answers. Maintaining a sense of humility allows you to be open to new information, evolving interpretations, and the possibility that your understanding of faith may continue to grow.

- **Embracing Mystery:** There are aspects of the divine that will always remain a mystery. Learning to be comfortable with the unknown allows you to appreciate the beauty and wonder of faith, even amidst unanswered questions.

By cultivating a faith that embraces doubt, weathers challenges, and finds balance between certainty and humility, we build a spiritual life that is both strong and adaptable. This resilient faith becomes a source of strength, comfort, and purpose throughout our journey.

5.1 Doubt and Deconstruction

One of the most significant challenges facing many Christians today, especially younger generations, is the process of doubt and faith deconstruction. This phenomenon, where believers question and sometimes dismantle their long-held beliefs, has become increasingly common in the digital age.

Apologetics serves a vital function in this context by:

1. Normalizing doubt: Apologists often emphasize that doubt is a normal part of faith development. They might point to biblical examples of doubters, like Thomas or Job, to show that questioning can be a pathway to deeper faith.
2. Providing intellectual support: By offering robust, reasoned arguments for core Christian beliefs, apologetics can provide a intellectual framework that supports faith during periods of questioning.
3. Addressing specific doubts: Whether it's questions about the reliability of Scripture, the problem of evil, or apparent contradictions in Christian doctrine, apologetics offers specific responses to common doubts.
4. Encouraging honest exploration: Rather than suppressing questions, apologetics encourages believers to explore their doubts openly, fostering an environment where faith can be tested and ultimately strengthened.
5. Offering a broader perspective: Apologetics can help doubters see beyond their immediate questions to the larger coherence and explanatory power of the Christian worldview.

5.2 Deepening Understanding

Beyond addressing doubts, apologetics plays a crucial role in deepening believers' understanding of their faith. This intellectual enrichment can lead to a more mature and resilient Christianity.

Key aspects of this include:

1. Theological depth: Apologetics often involves delving into complex theological concepts, helping believers move beyond surface-level understanding of their faith.
2. Historical context: By exploring the historical roots of Christianity and its doctrines, apologetics provides believers with a richer appreciation of their faith tradition.
3. Philosophical engagement: Apologetics introduces believers to philosophical concepts and arguments that can deepen their understanding of Christian truth claims.
4. Scientific literacy: In addressing questions at the intersection of faith and science, apologetics can help believers develop scientific literacy and appreciate how faith and reason can work together.
5. Cultural awareness: Apologetics often involves engaging with diverse worldviews, helping Christians understand and articulate their faith in a pluralistic context.

This deeper understanding serves multiple purposes:

- It equips believers to engage more confidently with non-believers, able to articulate and defend their faith more effectively.

- It helps Christians make more informed decisions in applying their faith to real-world situations.

- It fosters a more robust faith that can withstand intellectual challenges and personal crises.

5.3 Building Intellectual Virtues

Beyond providing information and arguments, apologetics plays a crucial role in cultivating intellectual virtues within the Christian community. These virtues are essential for navigating the complex landscape of faith in the modern world.

Some key intellectual virtues fostered by apologetics include:

1. Intellectual humility: Recognizing the limits of human knowledge and being open to correction and new understanding.
2. Critical thinking: Developing the ability to analyze arguments, evaluate evidence, and draw reasonable conclusions.
3. Intellectual courage: Being willing to ask difficult questions and follow the evidence where it leads, even when it challenges preconceptions.
4. Intellectual honesty: Committing to truthfulness in one's thinking and communication, acknowledging strengths in opposing arguments and weaknesses in one's own.
5. Curiosity: Cultivating a genuine interest in understanding different perspectives and exploring complex issues.

By fostering these virtues, apologetics not only strengthens individual faith but also contributes to a more thoughtful and engaging Christian presence in the wider culture.

Certainly. Let's continue with the next major section of the chapter.

6. Equipping for Evangelism

Apologetics plays a crucial role in equipping Christians for effective evangelism in the modern world. As society becomes increasingly secular and skeptical of religious claims, the ability to articulate and defend the faith has become an essential component of sharing the gospel.

6.1 Removing Intellectual Barriers

One of the primary functions of apologetics in evangelism is to address intellectual obstacles that may prevent people from considering the claims of Christianity.

1. Addressing Common Objections: Apologetics equips believers to respond to frequently raised objections to Christianity, such as:

○ The problem of evil and suffering

○ Perceived conflicts between science and faith

○ Questions about the reliability of the Bible

○ Issues with exclusive truth claims in a pluralistic world

2. Clarifying Misconceptions: Many people reject a caricature of Christianity rather than its true teachings. Apologetics helps to:

○ Explain complex doctrines in accessible ways

○ Differentiate between essential Christian beliefs and cultural accretions

○ Address historical misconceptions about the church's role in society

3. Demonstrating Rationality: In a culture that often views faith as opposed to reason, apologetics shows that:

○ Christian belief is intellectually defensible

○ Faith and reason are compatible

○ Christianity provides a coherent worldview that makes sense of human experience

6.2 Contextualizing the Gospel

Effective evangelism requires presenting the gospel in ways that resonate with the cultural context. Apologetics aids in this process by:

1. Cultural Analysis: Understanding the underlying beliefs, values, and assumptions of the target audience.
2. Finding Common Ground: Identifying shared concerns or values that can serve as bridges for gospel communication.
3. Addressing Felt Needs: Showing how the Christian message speaks to the deep existential questions and longings of contemporary people.
4. Translating Christian Concepts: Expressing biblical truths in language and thought forms that are accessible to those unfamiliar with Christian terminology.

6.3 Fostering Meaningful Dialogue

In an age of polarization and echo chambers, apologetics can promote genuine dialogue about matters of faith:

1. Active Listening: Training believers to truly hear and understand others' perspectives before responding.
2. Asking Good Questions: Using thoughtful questions to stimulate reflection and guide conversations towards deeper issues.
3. Respecting Disagreement: Modeling how to engage in respectful discourse with those who hold different views.
4. Building Relationships: Emphasizing the importance of genuine relationships in the process of evangelism, rather than seeing people as mere targets for conversion.

6.4 Integrating Reason and Personal Testimony

Effective apologetics in evangelism often combines rational arguments with personal experience:

1. Balancing Logic and Narrative: Showing how the intellectual case for Christianity aligns with the transformative power of personal faith.
2. Addressing Head and Heart: Recognizing that people are convinced not only by arguments but also by seeing authentic lived faith.
3. Sharing Personal Journey: Encouraging believers to articulate how apologetics has strengthened their own faith and addressed their own doubts.

6.5 Preparing for Follow-up

Apologetics in evangelism isn't just about initial conversations but also about being prepared for ongoing dialogue:

1. Anticipating Questions: Equipping believers to foresee and prepare for likely follow-up questions.
2. Providing Resources: Knowing where to direct people for deeper exploration of specific topics.
3. Connecting to Community: Recognizing when to invite seekers into Christian community for further discussion and experience of faith.

6.6 Adapting to Different Contexts

Apologetics in evangelism must be flexible, adapting to various settings:

1. One-on-One Conversations: Preparing for personal dialogues that may arise in everyday life.
2. Small Group Discussions: Equipping believers to facilitate thoughtful discussions in study groups or informal gatherings.
3. Public Forums: Preparing some Christians for more formal debates or presentations in academic or community settings.
4. Online Engagement: Developing strategies for effective apologetics in digital spaces, including social media and online forums.

6.7 Emphasizing the Goal

Throughout all these aspects, it's crucial to remember that the ultimate goal of apologetics in evangelism is not winning arguments, but winning people:

1. Maintaining Humility: Recognizing that while we can present arguments, ultimate conviction comes through the work of the Holy Spirit.
2. Focusing on Christ: Ensuring that all apologetic efforts ultimately point to the person and work of Jesus Christ.
3. Inviting Response: Learning how to move from intellectual discussions to personal invitation to faith in Christ.

By integrating apologetics into evangelism, Christians can engage in more effective and meaningful outreach, addressing both the intellectual and personal aspects of faith communication in the modern world.

7. Addressing Specific Contemporary Challenges

While we've covered broad cultural shifts, it's important to address some specific contemporary challenges that apologetics must engage with in the modern world. These issues require careful, nuanced responses that demonstrate both fidelity to Christian teachings and sensitivity to complex realities.

7.1 The Challenge of Scientism

Scientism, the view that science is the only reliable path to knowledge, has gained significant traction in modern society. Apologetics must address this challenge by:

1. Differentiating between science and scientism: Explaining how scientism is a philosophical position, not a scientific conclusion.
2. Highlighting the limitations of scientific inquiry: Demonstrating that there are questions (e.g., moral, aesthetic, and metaphysical) that science alone cannot answer.
3. Showcasing the compatibility of faith and science: Presenting examples of scientists who are believers and explaining how Christian theology has often supported scientific inquiry.
4. Addressing specific scientific challenges: Engaging with topics like evolution, the age of the earth, and neuroscience in ways that demonstrate thoughtful Christian responses.

7.2 The Problem of Evil and Suffering

This age-old challenge has taken on new dimensions in our globally connected world, where awareness of suffering is heightened. Apologetics must:

1. Provide logical responses: Explaining how the existence of evil doesn't logically preclude an all-powerful, all-loving God.

2. Offer pastoral care: Recognizing that this issue is often more emotional than intellectual, and responding with empathy and compassion.

3. Present a holistic Christian response: Showing how Christianity not only explains suffering but provides resources for facing it and working against it.

4. Address natural disasters and diseases: Engaging with hard questions about why God allows such events, especially in light of modern scientific understanding.

7.3 Religious Pluralism and the Exclusivity of Christ

In our diverse global society, Christianity's claims about Christ as the unique path to salvation face significant challenges. Apologetics must:

1. Explain the logic of Christian exclusivity: Showing why Christianity's truth claims necessarily exclude certain other beliefs.
2. Address charges of intolerance: Demonstrating how one can hold exclusive truth claims while still respecting and valuing people of other faiths.
3. Engage with other religions: Providing thoughtful comparisons that highlight both commonalities and crucial differences.
4. Present the inclusivity within Christian exclusivity: Explaining how Christianity teaches God's love for all people and desire for universal salvation.

7.4 Sexuality and Gender Issues

These topics have become highly contentious in modern society. Apologetics must navigate these waters carefully by:

1. Clearly articulating traditional Christian sexual ethics: Explaining the biblical and theological foundations for these views.

2. Addressing charges of bigotry: Showing how Christian sexual ethics are based on a positive view of human sexuality and not on hatred or fear.

3. Engaging with personal experiences: Recognizing the complex realities of human sexuality and gender identity while maintaining biblical standards.

4. Promoting compassion and dignity: Emphasizing the Christian call to love and respect all people, regardless of sexual orientation or gender identity.

7.5 The Challenge of Postmodern Relativism

While we touched on postmodernism earlier, its impact on truth claims deserves specific attention. Apologetics must:

1. Expose the self-defeating nature of extreme relativism: Demonstrating how absolute relativism contradicts itself.
2. Acknowledge valid postmodern insights: Showing how Christianity can incorporate valuable postmodern emphases on context and perspective.
3. Present Christianity as a meta-narrative: Offering the Christian worldview as a comprehensive story that makes sense of human experience.
4. Engage with lived experiences: Showing how Christian truth claims connect with and explain real-life experiences.

7.6 Environmental Concerns

With growing awareness of environmental issues, apologetics must address how Christianity relates to care for creation:

1. Present a biblical theology of creation care: Showing how stewardship of the environment is a Christian responsibility.
2. Address misconceptions: Countering the idea that Christianity is inherently anti-environmental due to concepts like dominion.
3. Engage with scientific data: Demonstrating a willingness to take seriously the scientific consensus on issues like climate change.
4. Offer a Christian perspective on environmental ethics: Showing how Christian principles can inform approaches to environmental issues.

7.7 Artificial Intelligence and Transhumanism

As technology advances, new philosophical and ethical questions arise. Apologetics must:

1. Engage with questions of consciousness and the soul: Addressing how Christian anthropology relates to AI development.
2. Discuss the ethics of human enhancement: Offering Christian perspectives on the promises and perils of transhumanist ambitions.
3. Address existential questions: Exploring how Christianity speaks to fears and hopes raised by rapid technological change.
4. Present a vision of human flourishing: Contrasting Christian views of what it means to be human with techno-utopian visions.

8. Developing Effective Apologetic Methods

To address the diverse challenges of the modern world, Christians need to develop effective apologetic methods that are both faithful to the truth of Christianity and relevant to contemporary audiences. This section explores various approaches and strategies for effective apologetics.

8.1 The Importance of Listening

Before presenting arguments, effective apologetics begins with careful listening:

1. Understanding the real question: Often, the stated objection isn't the real issue. Listening helps uncover underlying concerns.
2. Identifying worldview assumptions: Careful listening reveals the foundational beliefs shaping a person's objections or questions.
3. Building rapport: Genuine listening demonstrates respect and opens doors for meaningful dialogue.
4. Tailoring the approach: Understanding the individual's background and concerns allows for a more personalized apologetic response.

8.2 Employing the Socratic Method

The Socratic method of asking probing questions can be a powerful apologetic tool:

1. Exposing inconsistencies: Thoughtful questions can reveal inconsistencies in non-Christian worldviews.
2. Encouraging self-reflection: Questions can lead people to examine their own beliefs more critically.
3. Guiding the conversation: Strategic questions can steer the discussion towards key issues.
4. Avoiding defensiveness: Questions can present challenges to other viewpoints without seeming confrontational.

8.3 Utilizing Cumulative Case Arguments

Rather than relying on a single, knockdown argument, effective apologetics often builds a cumulative case:

1. Combining multiple lines of evidence: Presenting various arguments that together make a compelling case for Christianity.
2. Addressing different aspects: Using diverse arguments to speak to both rational and experiential aspects of faith.
3. Overcoming objections: A cumulative case can be robust even if individual arguments are not definitive.
4. Appealing to different personalities: Various arguments may resonate differently with different individuals.

8.4 Narrative Apologetics

Recognizing the power of story in human understanding, narrative apologetics has gained prominence:

1. Using biblical narratives: Showing how biblical stories speak to contemporary issues and existential questions.
2. Sharing personal testimonies: Demonstrating the transformative power of faith through personal stories.
3. Engaging with cultural narratives: Showing how the Christian story provides a more compelling narrative than competing worldviews.
4. Addressing the heart and imagination: Recognizing that people are moved not just by arguments but by compelling visions of reality.

8.5 Presuppositional Apologetics

This approach focuses on exposing and challenging the foundational assumptions of non-Christian worldviews:

1. Revealing underlying beliefs: Helping people recognize the presuppositions that shape their thinking.
2. Demonstrating the necessity of God: Arguing that things we take for granted (like logic or morality) only make sense within a theistic framework.
3. Exposing the inconsistency of unbelief: Showing how non-Christian worldviews borrow from Christian assumptions.
4. Presenting Christianity as a coherent worldview: Demonstrating how Christianity provides a consistent foundation for knowledge and ethics.

8.6 Evidential Apologetics

This method focuses on presenting empirical evidence for the truth of Christianity:

1. Historical evidence: Presenting archaeological and textual evidence for the reliability of the Bible.
2. Scientific evidence: Discussing how scientific discoveries align with or point to a Creator.
3. Experiential evidence: Sharing testimonies of answered prayer or miraculous events.
4. Philosophical evidence: Offering logical arguments for God's existence or the resurrection of Jesus.

8.7 Cultural Apologetics

This approach seeks to demonstrate the relevance and attractiveness of Christianity to contemporary culture:

1. Engaging with the arts: Showing how Christian themes resonate in literature, film, and music.
2. Addressing cultural longings: Demonstrating how Christianity speaks to deep human desires for meaning, justice, and love.
3. Critiquing cultural idols: Exposing the inadequacies of modern substitutes for God (e.g., consumerism, individualism).
4. Presenting Christian alternatives: Offering a vision of how Christianity can positively shape culture and society.

8.8 Interdisciplinary Apologetics

Recognizing the complexity of modern challenges, this approach draws on multiple disciplines:

1. Integrating sciences: Showing how insights from physics, biology, and psychology align with Christian truth claims.
2. Incorporating philosophy: Using philosophical reasoning to support Christian doctrines and ethics.
3. Engaging with social sciences: Drawing on sociology and anthropology to demonstrate the social benefits of Christianity.
4. Utilizing technology: Employing digital tools and platforms for apologetic engagement.

8.9 Practical Application

Effective apologetics must move beyond theory to practical application:

1. Training programs: Developing curriculum for churches and schools to equip believers in apologetics.
2. Media engagement: Creating podcasts, videos, and social media content to reach broader audiences.
3. Community outreach: Organizing events and discussion groups to engage with local communities.
4. Mentoring: Establishing mentoring relationships to develop the next generation of apologists.

Common Q&A: Exploring Faith Through Apologetics

Comoom (Let's talk!): Here are some common questions and answers regarding apologetics, the study of defending religious beliefs:

Q: What's the point of apologetics? Don't I just need faith?

A: Apologetics isn't about forcing faith on others. It's about equipping yourself to:

- **Strengthen your own faith:** By exploring the reasons behind your beliefs, your faith can become more grounded.

- **Address doubts and challenges:** Everyone has questions. Apologetics can help you find answers and navigate challenges to your faith.

- **Engage in respectful conversations:** Apologetics equips you to explain your faith clearly and thoughtfully to others, even if they have different beliefs.

Q: Are there different approaches to apologetics?
A: Yes! Here are a few common ones:

- **Classical Apologetics:** Uses logic, philosophy, and evidence (like historical records) to establish God's existence and the truth claims of a religion.

- **Evidential Apologetics:** Focuses on using scientific evidence, historical data, and philosophical arguments to support religious beliefs.

- **Experiential Apologetics:** Emphasizes the importance of personal experiences and the transformative power of faith.

Q: Isn't apologetics just about using fancy arguments to win debates?

A: Not necessarily. Apologetics should be about genuine understanding and respectful dialogue. While well-reasoned arguments are helpful, focusing solely on "winning" discussions can be counterproductive.

Q: I don't feel comfortable arguing about religion. Is apologetics still for me?

A: Absolutely! Apologetics isn't just about formal debates. It's also about developing your own understanding and being able to answer questions or explain your beliefs to others in a clear and confident way.

Q: How can I develop my apologetic skills?

A: Here are some tips:

- **Solidify your own beliefs:** Clearly understand the core tenets of your faith tradition.

- **Explore different apologetic approaches:** Learn about the various ways people defend their faith.

- **Practice respectful dialogue:** Talk to fellow believers and people of other faiths, focusing on understanding different perspectives.

- **Develop your communication skills:** Be able to articulate your beliefs clearly and concisely.

● **Be open to learning:** Embrace a growth mindset and be willing to explore new ideas.

Remember, apologetics is a journey, not a destination. It's about seeking truth, strengthening your faith, and engaging in meaningful conversations about what matters most.

Christianity for the Non-Believer

Here are some more questions people who don't currently believe in Christianity might have:

Q: Isn't the Bible full of contradictions and historical inaccuracies?

A: The Bible is a collection of writings spanning centuries and genres. There can be seemingly contradictory passages due to historical context, translation issues, or literary styles. Many Christians believe the Bible's core message remains consistent despite these variations. There's also ongoing scholarly debate about the Bible's historical accuracy. Some Christians view the Bible as a completely literal and accurate historical record, while others see it as a divinely inspired but not always literal guide.

Q: How can I be sure Jesus actually existed?

A: There's no single, definitive piece of evidence that proves Jesus' existence outside the Bible. However, some historians consider writings by Josephus and Tacitus, Roman historians from the 1st century AD, to be extra-Biblical references to Jesus. The strength of the evidence for Jesus' existence is a matter of ongoing debate among scholars. Ultimately, faith plays a role in believing in Jesus' historical reality.

Q: What about other religions? Christianity seems like just one option among many.

A: Christianity acknowledges the existence of other faiths. Some Christians believe Christianity fulfills the truths found in other religions, while others see it as the one true path. Interfaith dialogue is an ongoing field of study that explores the common ground and unique aspects of various religions.

Q: I'm worried about making a lifelong commitment. Can I just try out Christianity for a while?

A: Absolutely! Many churches offer programs or classes for seekers who want to learn more about Christianity before fully committing. You can explore Christian teachings, attend services, and talk to believers without feeling pressured to convert.

Q: Does Christianity require me to give up everything I enjoy?

A: Christianity emphasizes living a moral life, but it doesn't mean giving up all enjoyment. Different denominations have varying views on specific practices, but most encourage moderation and responsible living. **Q: What about the role of the Church? Isn't it filled with hypocrisy and scandals?**

A: The Church is made up of humans, and humans are imperfect. Throughout history, there have been issues within the Church, and some Christians have acted in ways that contradict their faith. However, many Christians believe the Church is still essential for spiritual growth, community, and the spread of their faith.

Q: Does Christianity emphasize blind obedience? Can't I question things?

A: The Bible encourages asking questions and grappling with doubt. Many Christian thinkers and theologians have a rich history of wrestling with complex issues. While core beliefs are important, blind obedience isn't a core Christian value.

Q: What if I don't feel a strong emotional connection to God? Does that mean I'm not a true Christian?

A: Faith can look different for different people. Not everyone experiences a dramatic conversion or feels a constant emotional connection to God. Some Christians focus on intellectual understanding, while others emphasize practicing their faith through good works and living a moral life.

Q: Isn't Christianity mostly about following rules and avoiding sin?

A: While avoiding sin is important, Christianity is ultimately about grace and love. Christians believe that everyone sins, but through faith in Jesus Christ, they can be forgiven and experience God's love.

Q: I'm worried about what happens after death. Does Christianity offer any answers?

A: Christianity offers the concept of an afterlife, with eternal life in heaven for those who believe in Jesus Christ. There are different views on the nature of heaven and hell, but the core belief is that death is not the end.

Digging Deeper: Christianity for the Non-Believer

Here are some more questions delving into specific aspects of Christianity:

Science and Faith:

- **Q: Can't evolution and creationism coexist? How do Christians view the origins of life?**

There isn't a single Christian view on origins. Some believe in a literal interpretation of creation in Genesis, while others see it as a metaphor or reconcile it with the theory of evolution through concepts like "theistic evolution."

Christian Practices:

- **Q: Why do Christians go to church? What happens during a service?**

Church attendance is a way for Christians to worship God, connect with other believers, and learn from religious teachings. Services vary by denomination but often involve prayer, scripture readings, music, and a sermon.

- **Q: What are the sacraments? Why are they important?**

Sacraments are rituals believed to be sacred acts instituted by Jesus. The two most common sacraments are baptism (symbolic cleansing and initiation) and communion (symbolic sharing of the body and blood of Christ). Their importance and interpretation vary among denominations.

Christian Living:

- **Q: How does Christianity define sin? How can I avoid sinning?**

Sin is generally understood as breaking God's law or rebelling against God's will. Christians strive to live morally and avoid actions that harm themselves or others. Different denominations have varying lists of specific sins.

- **Q: What about social justice issues? Does Christianity have a stance on poverty, war, or LGBTQ+ rights?**

The Bible offers guidance on social issues, but interpretations and applications vary. Some Christians are actively involved in social justice movements, while others focus more on personal salvation.

The Bible:

• Q: How can I interpret the Bible for myself? Are there different methods?

There are various approaches to interpreting the Bible. Some emphasize the literal meaning, while others consider historical context, literary style, and the Bible's overall message.

• Q: Are there any historical figures I can learn about to see faith in action?

Christianity has a rich history filled with inspiring figures. You can explore missionaries, martyrs, social reformers, theologians, and everyday Christians who lived out their faith in remarkable ways.

Christianity's Impact on the World:

• Q: How has Christianity influenced history and culture?

Christianity has profoundly shaped Western art, music, literature, law, ethics, and social institutions. The impact extends to education, healthcare, and charitable works around the world.

• Q: Christianity has been used to justify violence and oppression throughout history. How do you reconcile that with its message of love?

This is a difficult question many Christians grapple with. Some argue these acts contradict true Christian teachings, while others acknowledge the misuse of faith for power. Understanding historical context and ongoing debates about Christian ethics is crucial.

Denominational Differences:

- **Q: What are the major Christian denominations, and how do they differ?**

Christianity has many branches, each with distinct beliefs and practices. Major denominations include Catholicism, Protestantism (further divided into Lutherans, Methodists, Baptists, etc.), Eastern Orthodoxy, and Pentecostalism. Differences lie in church structures, sacraments, interpretations of scripture, and social stances.

The Future of Christianity:

- **Q: How is Christianity adapting to a changing world? Is it losing relevance?**

Christianity is a global religion constantly evolving. Some denominations are more conservative, while others embrace social change and theological interpretations. The future of Christianity depends on how it adapts to new challenges and opportunities.

Personal and Philosophical Questions:

- **Q: If God is all-knowing, can we have free will? Isn't everything predetermined?**

This is a complex theological debate. Some believe God grants us free will, while others see our choices as part of God's overall plan. Reconciling these concepts is an ongoing challenge.

- **Q: Does Christianity offer answers to the meaning of life? What is our purpose?**

Many Christians believe life's purpose is to love God, live according to his teachings, and ultimately experience eternal life. Finding meaning can also involve serving others, pursuing purpose-driven work, and leaving a positive impact on the world.

Christian Theology:

● Q: What is the Trinity? How can God be one and three at the same time?

The Trinity is the doctrine that God exists as three persons (Father, Son, and Holy Spirit) in one Godhead. It's a complex concept with various explanations throughout Christian history. Understanding it involves grappling with philosophical and theological ideas about God's nature.

● Q: What is predestination? Does it mean some are chosen for heaven and others for hell?

Predestination is the belief that God predetermines salvation or damnation. There are different interpretations: some see it as God's sovereign choice, while others believe it hinges on human free will and response to God's grace.

● Q: What is the role of the Holy Spirit? How do Christians experience it?

The Holy Spirit is believed to be the presence and power of God at work in the world. Christians may experience it in various ways, such as a sense of guidance, conviction, or empowerment for ministry and good works.

Christian Practices:

• Q: What is prayer? How do Christians approach prayer?

Prayer is communication with God. Christians pray for various reasons, including expressing gratitude, seeking guidance, confessing sin, and interceding for others. Prayer styles vary, from formal liturgies to personal, heartfelt conversations with God.

• Q: What about worship? Why is it important for Christians?

Worship is the act of giving praise, reverence, and adoration to God. It can be individual or communal, involving elements like music, prayer, scripture reading, and sacraments. Worship expresses love for God and strengthens believers' faith.

• Q: Why do some Christians tithe (give 10% of their income) to the church?

Tithing is a practice based on Old Testament teachings, though interpretations vary. Some see it as an obligation, while others view it as a voluntary expression of gratitude and commitment to supporting the church's mission.

Christian Living:

• Q: How can I cultivate a Christ-like character?

Christians strive to live according to the teachings of Jesus, emphasizing love, forgiveness, compassion, humility, and service to others. Developing Christ-like character involves studying scripture, prayer, and actively seeking opportunities to embody these values.

- **Q: What about forgiveness? How can I forgive someone who has wronged me?**

Forgiveness is a core Christian teaching. While it doesn't mean forgetting the offense, it involves letting go of resentment and choosing not to seek revenge. Prayer and seeking support from Christian community can aid the forgiveness process.

The Bible:

- **Q: What are the different genres of writing found in the Bible? How does this affect interpretation?**

The Bible contains various genres like history, poetry, law, prophecy, and letters. Understanding the genre helps with interpretation, as poetry shouldn't be taken literally like historical accounts.

- **Q: Are there any archaeological discoveries that confirm the Bible's accuracy?**

Archaeology has unearthed artifacts and inscriptions that corroborate some biblical events and places. However, archaeology doesn't necessarily prove the Bible's supernatural elements or theological claims.

Engaging with Christianity:

- **Q: How can I find a church that aligns with my beliefs?**

Many denominations exist within Christianity. Researching different churches' doctrines, practices, and worship styles can help you find a community that resonates with you. Attending services and talking to church members can also be helpful.

● Q: How can I share my faith with others without being pushy?

Christians are called to share their faith, but it should be done with respect and love. Live out your faith through your actions, be open to conversations, and answer questions honestly. Ultimately, people make their own choices about faith.

● Q: What are some common misconceptions about Christianity?

There are many stereotypes about Christians, such as being judgmental, anti-science, or literal interpreters of the Bible. Engaging with Christians and learning about their diverse beliefs can dispel these misconceptions.

Christianity and Other Worldviews:

- **Q: How does Christianity view other religions? Are they all paths to the same God?**

Christian views on other religions vary. Some believe Christianity is the only true path, while others see elements of truth in various faiths. Interfaith dialogue explores common ground and fosters mutual understanding.

- **Q: What about atheism and agnosticism? How does Christianity respond to those who don't believe in God?**

Atheism is the disbelief in God, while agnosticism is the position that the existence of God is unknown or unknowable. Christians may engage in respectful dialogue to share their faith, but ultimately, they believe in the freedom of individual belief.

- **Q: Christianity seems patriarchal. What is the role of women in Christianity?**

The Bible contains patriarchal structures, but interpretations and roles for women vary across denominations. Many denominations now have women in leadership roles, and there's ongoing discussion about gender equality within Christianity.

Christian Mysticism and Spirituality:

- **Q: What is Christian mysticism? How do some Christians experience a deeper connection with God?**

Christian mysticism explores a more personal, intimate encounter with God beyond religious rituals and intellectual understanding. Mystics may describe visions, feelings of oneness with God, or a deep sense of divine presence.

● Q: What are spiritual disciplines? How can they help me grow in my faith?

Spiritual disciplines are practices intended to cultivate a closer relationship with God. They can include prayer, meditation, scripture study, fasting, and acts of service. These practices can vary depending on denomination and personal preference.

● Q: Does Christianity have any practices of contemplation or meditation?

Yes, some Christian traditions incorporate contemplative prayer or meditation practices. These practices involve focusing on God, quieting the mind, and opening oneself to God's presence.

Christian Art, Music, and Literature:

● Q: How has Christianity influenced art, music, and literature?

Christianity has profoundly shaped these artistic expressions. From grand cathedrals to sacred music to classic novels exploring faith and morality, Christian themes have permeated artistic endeavors for centuries.

● Q: Are there any Christian artists, musicians, or authors whose work I can explore?

There are countless! Depending on your interests, you could explore artists like Michelangelo and El Greco, musicians like Bach and Handel, or authors like C.S. Lewis and Dostoevsky.

- **Q: How can engaging with Christian art, music, and literature enrich my understanding of faith?**

These artistic expressions can offer unique perspectives on faith, evoke emotions, and spark deeper contemplation of religious themes.

Christianity and Social Issues:

• Q: What is the Christian stance on social justice issues like poverty, homelessness, and racial inequality?

The Bible emphasizes caring for the poor and marginalized. Christians are called to work for justice and compassion in society. Denominations may have varying approaches and focuses on specific social issues.

• Q: How does Christianity view environmental stewardship? Does the Bible have anything to say about caring for the Earth?

The Bible speaks of creation care and human responsibility for the Earth. Many Christians are actively involved in environmental movements, believing they align with their faith's values.

• Q: What is the Christian perspective on war and violence? When is violence justified, if ever?

The Bible contains passages that seem to condone violence, while others promote peacemaking. Christians wrestle with this tension, advocating for peace while acknowledging the complexities of a fallen world where violence may be a regrettable necessity in some situations.

Christian Denominations:

• Q: What are some lesser-known Christian denominations, and what makes them unique?

Beyond major denominations, there are numerous Christian traditions with distinct beliefs and practices. Exploring lesser-known denominations can broaden your understanding of the Christian spectrum.

• Q: How do Christians from different denominations view each other? Is there ecumenical cooperation?

There's a spectrum of views. Some denominations see themselves as the one true church, while others emphasize common ground and engage in ecumenical efforts like joint projects or dialogues.

• Q: How have Christian denominations changed throughout history? Have there been major schisms or reforms?

Christianity has a long history of splits and reforms. Understanding these historical developments can shed light on the diversity of Christian beliefs today.

Christianity and Science:

● Q: Can a person be both a scientist and a Christian? Are science and faith inherently opposed?

Many prominent scientists throughout history have reconciled their faith with scientific discoveries. Some Christians see science and faith as complementary ways of understanding the world, while others view them as separate domains.

● Q: How do Christians approach controversial topics like evolution or human origins?

There isn't one Christian view on these issues. Some believe in strict creationism, while others see evolution as compatible with their faith. The approach often hinges on how literally one interprets the Bible's creation narratives.

● Q: Does Christianity have anything to say about artificial intelligence or biotechnology? Are there any ethical concerns?

These are emerging fields. Some Christians are optimistic about the potential benefits, while others raise ethical concerns about the potential misuse of technology or its impact on human identity.

Christian Eschatology (End Times):

● Q: What does the Bible say about the end times? What are some different Christian interpretations?

The Bible includes passages about the return of Christ, judgment, and a new heaven and new earth. Interpretations vary widely, with some Christians believing in a literal rapture and millennial reign of Christ, while others view these concepts symbolically.

- **Q: How do Christians approach death and the afterlife?**

Christians generally believe in an afterlife, with eternal life in heaven for believers and eternal separation from God in hell for those who reject him. There are also varying views on the nature of heaven and hell, and some denominations emphasize a state of purgatory for purification before entering heaven.

Christian Ethics:

- **Q: Does Christianity offer a clear moral code? How do Christians make ethical decisions?**

The Bible provides moral guidelines, but navigating complex situations requires prayer, reflection, and applying biblical principles to contemporary issues. Christian ethics emphasize virtues like love, honesty, justice, and compassion.

- **Q: What about bioethics? How does Christianity view issues like abortion, euthanasia, or genetic engineering?**

These issues raise complex ethical dilemmas. Christians may have differing viewpoints based on their interpretation of scripture and their understanding of human life and dignity.

Christian Holidays and Traditions:

- **Q: What are the major Christian holidays, and what is their significance?**

Christmas celebrates Jesus' birth, Easter commemorates his death and resurrection, and Pentecost celebrates the descent of the Holy Spirit. These holidays hold deep theological meaning and are also celebrated through traditions like gift-giving, special meals, and church services.

- **Q: What are some lesser-known Christian traditions, and how do they vary across cultures?**

Christianity has been adapted and expressed in diverse ways across cultures. Exploring lesser-known traditions can broaden your understanding of how faith is practiced around the world.

Christianity and Personal Growth:

- **Q: How can Christianity help me become a better person?**

Christian teachings emphasize values like love, forgiveness, and service to others. Following these principles can foster personal growth, develop a strong moral compass, and contribute positively to society.

- **Q: What resources are available to help me learn more about Christianity?**

Numerous resources exist! The Bible itself is the foundation, but commentaries, devotional books, online resources, and courses can provide deeper understanding. Talking to Christians and attending church services can also be invaluable.

Christianity and the Individual:

- **Q: How can I know if I'm a true Christian? Do I need a special experience (like a conversion)?**

There's no single test for being a true Christian. It's more about a genuine desire to follow Jesus' teachings, live a moral life, and grow in your faith. Conversion experiences vary, but ultimately, faith is a personal journey.

- **Q: What does it mean to have a relationship with God? How can I cultivate that?**

A relationship with God is about communication and connection. Prayer, meditation, studying scripture, and participating in religious activities can help cultivate this relationship. It's a lifelong process with periods of growth and challenges.

- **Q: I doubt my faith sometimes. Is that normal?**

Absolutely! Doubt is a natural part of faith. Even prominent figures in the Bible wrestled with doubt. The key is to keep seeking answers, engage with your doubts honestly, and allow your faith to mature.

Christianity and Society:

● Q: How can I be a Christian in a secular world?

Living a Christian life in a secular world can be challenging. Focus on living your values, share your faith with respect, and find a Christian community for support and encouragement.

● Q: What about social justice issues? How can I be a voice for the voiceless?

Many Christians are actively involved in social justice movements. Find causes that resonate with your faith and use your voice and actions to advocate for a more just and compassionate world.

● Q: How can I share my faith with others without being pushy?

Live your faith authentically, be open to conversations, and answer questions honestly. Ultimately, respect others' choices while offering your own perspective with love and kindness.

The Bible and Interpretation:

● Q: How can I be sure I'm interpreting the Bible correctly?

There's no single "correct" interpretation. Consider historical context, literary style, and the overall message of the Bible. Use commentaries, study guides, and discussions with trusted Christians to gain different perspectives.

● Q: What about difficult passages in the Bible? How do I reconcile them with my values?

The Bible contains passages that seem contradictory or morally troubling. Seek guidance from scholars, pastors, or theologians. Consider the historical context, the original language, and how the passage aligns with the Bible's overall message.

● Q: Are there any resources to help me study the Bible more deeply?

There are many resources available! Bible study guides, commentaries, online courses, and theological books can provide deeper understanding. Consider joining a Bible study group at a church for community learning.

Christian Spirituality:

● Q: What are spiritual gifts? How can I identify mine?

The Bible mentions spiritual gifts, which are special abilities bestowed by the Holy Spirit to serve the church and glorify God. These can include teaching, prophecy, encouragement, or acts of service. Christians can explore their gifts through prayer, reflection, and serving within the church.

● Q: What is Christian mysticism? How do some Christians experience a deeper connection with God?

Christian mysticism goes beyond rituals and intellectual understanding. It involves a direct, personal encounter with God, often described as visions, feelings of oneness with God, or a profound sense of divine presence. Mystics may use practices like prayer, meditation, and contemplation to cultivate this connection.

● Q: What is discernment of spirits? How can I tell if a spiritual experience is from God?

Discernment of spirits is the ability to distinguish between genuine spiritual experiences and those that may have other origins. Christians may use scripture, prayer, and guidance from trusted spiritual leaders to discern the source of an experience.

Christian Practices:

● Q: What is spiritual warfare? How do Christians combat evil?

Spiritual warfare is the belief that Christians are engaged in a spiritual battle against demonic forces. It's not about physical violence, but about resisting evil through prayer, living a holy life, and proclaiming the truth of the Gospel.

- **Q: What about miracles? Do they still happen today?**

The Bible recounts many miracles. Belief in modern-day miracles varies among Christians. Some emphasize the importance of seeking God's will through prayer, while others may believe God continues to work miraculously in the world.

- **Q: What is speaking in tongues? Is it a necessary part of the Christian experience?**

Speaking in tongues is a phenomenon mentioned in the Bible where someone speaks in an unknown language, believed to be a gift of the Holy Spirit. Not all Christians believe in or experience speaking in tongues, and it's not considered essential for salvation.

Christian Denominations and Practices:

- **Q: What are some lesser-known Christian practices like glossolalia (speaking in tongues) or holy laughter?**

These are practices associated with certain Pentecostal and charismatic denominations. Glossolalia is speaking in tongues, while holy laughter is an uncontrollable laughter believed to be a manifestation of the Holy Spirit. These practices are not universal within Christianity.

- **Q: How do some Christian denominations view Mary, the mother of Jesus?**

Views on Mary vary. Catholics and Orthodox Christians venerate her and see her as interceding for believers. Protestant denominations generally focus more on Jesus' direct relationship with God.

● Q: What are Christian sacraments, and how do they differ between denominations?

Sacraments are rituals believed to be sacred acts instituted by Jesus. Baptism and communion are the most common. Their interpretation and significance vary among denominations. Some see them as symbolic acts, while others believe they transmit God's grace.

Origins and Early Christianity:

- **Q: What were the historical circumstances surrounding the rise of Christianity?**

Christianity emerged in the Roman Empire during a time of social unrest, religious diversity, and a search for meaning. Jewish messianic expectations and Greek philosophy influenced early Christian thought.

- **Q: Who were the early Church Fathers? What role did they play in shaping Christianity?**

Early Church Fathers were influential theologians and writers who defended and defined Christian doctrines in the centuries after Jesus. They addressed heresies, interpreted scripture, and established core Christian beliefs. Figures like Augustine and Aquinas continue to be studied today.

- **Q: How did Christianity spread throughout the Roman Empire?**

The spread of Christianity is attributed to various factors, including the message of hope and salvation, the work of missionaries, the persecution of early Christians (which paradoxically led to wider awareness), and the eventual adoption of Christianity by the Roman emperor Constantine in the 4th century.

The Middle Ages and Reformation:

- **Q: What was the role of the Catholic Church in the Middle Ages?**

The Catholic Church held immense political and social power in medieval Europe. It preserved and transmitted classical learning, built cathedrals, and played a significant role in people's lives. However, there were also criticisms of corruption and abuses of power within the Church.

- **Q: What caused the Protestant Reformation? What were the key figures and ideas?**

The Reformation was a 16th-century movement that challenged the Catholic Church's authority and practices. Figures like Martin Luther and John Calvin emphasized the importance of scripture, individual faith, and justification by faith alone, leading to the establishment of Protestant denominations.

Christianity and the Modern World:

- **Q: How did Christianity influence the development of Western civilization?**

Christianity's impact is vast, shaping art, literature, law, ethics, and social institutions. It inspired movements for social reform, education, and healthcare. Western values like individual rights and democracy have roots in Christian thought.

- **Q: How is Christianity adapting to the challenges of the modern world?**

Christianity faces challenges like secularization, scientific advancements, and ethical dilemmas. Some denominations embrace social change and theological interpretations, while others maintain more conservative stances. The future of Christianity depends on its ability to engage with contemporary issues while staying true to its core message.

Studying Christian History:

• **Q: What are some resources for learning more about
Christian history?**

Numerous resources exist! Books on church history,
documentaries, online courses, and visiting historical sites like
cathedrals or monasteries can provide an immersive experience.
Reading primary sources like writings of Church Fathers can offer
firsthand perspectives.

Conclusion

Christianity is a vast and multifaceted tapestry woven from history, theology, practices, and personal experiences. This FAQ has explored numerous threads, offering a glimpse into the richness and complexity of this faith tradition.

As you delve deeper, remember there are no simple answers. Christianity is a journey of exploration, questioning, and growth. Here are some concluding thoughts to guide you further:

- **Embrace the journey:** Christianity is a lifelong exploration. Don't be afraid to ask questions, have doubts, and seek guidance.

- **Engage with diverse perspectives:** Christianity is not monolithic. Explore different denominations, theological views, and cultural expressions of faith.

- **Experience it firsthand:** Attend a church service, talk to Christians, or read inspirational stories. A genuine encounter can deepen your understanding.

- **Respectful dialogue:** Engage with others, even those who disagree. Share your faith with respect and love, and be open to learning from others' perspectives.

- **Live your values:** Ultimately, Christianity is about putting your faith into action. Live a life that reflects love, compassion, and service to others.

Whether you choose to embrace Christianity or not, this exploration has hopefully unveiled its profound impact on the world and the potential it holds for personal growth and meaning. The choice to believe is yours, but the journey of discovery is a valuable one in itself.

Conclusion

Christianity is a vast and multifaceted tapestry woven from history, theology, practices, and personal experiences. This book has explored numerous threads, offering a glimpse into the richness and complexity of this faith tradition.

As you delve deeper, remember there are no simple answers. Christianity is a journey of exploration, questioning, and growth. Here are some concluding thoughts to guide you further:

- **Embrace the journey:** Christianity is a lifelong exploration. Don't be afraid to ask questions, have doubts, and seek guidance.

- **Engage with diverse perspectives:** Christianity is not monolithic. Explore different denominations, theological views, and cultural expressions of faith.

- **Experience it firsthand:** Attend a church service, talk to Christians, or read inspirational stories. A genuine encounter can deepen your understanding.

- **Respectful dialogue:** Engage with others, even those who disagree. Share your faith with respect and love, and be open to learning from others' perspectives.

- **Live your values:** Ultimately, Christianity is about putting your faith into action. Live a life that reflects love, compassion, and service to others.

Whether you choose to embrace Christianity or not, this exploration has hopefully unveiled its profound impact on the world and the potential it holds for personal growth and meaning. The choice to believe is yours, but the journey of discovery is a valuable one in itself.

Looking to delve deeper?

I, Daniel Sanjurjo, have written other books exploring various aspects of the Bible. If you enjoyed this exploration, you might find them enriching additions to your bookshelf.

Remember, the most important aspect of faith is a personal connection. May your exploration continue, and may you find meaning and purpose on your journey.

Don't miss out!

Visit the website below and you can sign up to receive emails whenever Daniel Sanjurjo publishes a new book. There's no charge and no obligation.

https://books2read.com/r/B-A-WQHBB-IJMOD

BOOKS2READ

Connecting independent readers to independent writers.

About the Author

Daniel Sanjurjo is a dedicated author of books on the Bible and Christianity. His works focus on exploring and explaining the depths of faith, making complex theological concepts accessible and engaging for all readers. Daniel's passion for sharing knowledge and understanding of Christian beliefs shines through in every page he writes.

Read more at https://www.linkedin.com/in/daniel-sanjurjo/.